# IN A DISTANT ISLE

*for*
**ELMA**

# IN A DISTANT ISLE
## The Orkney Background
of
Edwin Muir

## GEORGE MARSHALL

SCOTTISH ACADEMIC PRESS
EDINBURGH
1987

Published by
Scottish Academic Press Ltd.
33 Montgomery Street
Edinburgh EH7 5JX


First published 1987
ISBN 0 7073 0469 5

Scottish Academic Press
acknowledges subsidy from the Scottish Arts Council
towards the publication of this volume




Printed in Great Britain by
Bell and Bain Ltd., Glasgow
Typeset at Oxford University Computing Service
from a machine-readable text
prepared by Wilma S. Mack, Dollar

# CONTENTS

# ACKNOWLEDGEMENTS

MY THANKS are due to Faber and Faber for permission to quote from Muir's *Collected Poems* and to the Hogarth Press for permission to quote from *An Autobiography*, *Essays in Literature*, *The Estate of Poetry* and *Selected Letters of Edwin Muir*.

Thanks are due also to Professor Norman Sherry for encouraging me to undertake the writing of this book and to those others who gave valuable help and advice while I was writing it: Miss Alison Fraser, Dr Judith George, Miss Deirdre Keaney, Mrs Elma Marshall, Mrs Sylvia Sherry, Mr W.P.L. Thomson, and the staff of the Orkney Library.

Finally, like all who in recent years have explored the material held in the Orkney Archives, I owe a great debt of gratitude to the late Ernest W. Marwick without whose sensitive and imaginative recording this book could not have been written.

GEORGE MARSHALL
*Durham, 1986*

# INTRODUCTION

THE POETRY of Edwin Muir has come to be regarded as among the most important produced this century. Muir's admirers can, without self-consciousness, equate his poems with those of Yeats, Eliot, Pound, Auden and Graves. The themes of his poems are often similar to theirs. In particular he is, like most of the leading poets of his time, acutely aware of the isolation of the individual in modern society.

But Muir's voice is a distinctive one. The distinctiveness is, of course, partly a matter of personality: not for nothing did his friends at school remember him as "different". But he is different, too, because of his background. Possibly alone among the major British poets of this century, Muir grew up in a rural, traditional, isolated, and self-contained community, following a way of life on which the Industrial Revolution was only just beginning to have an effect. To his subsequent experience of living in Glasgow, London, Prague and Rome, Muir brought a singular innocence.

Edwin Muir spent the first fifteen years of his life in the Orkney Islands—a small, rather remote group of islands off the north coast of Scotland. He did not forget those years. Indeed, he came increasingly to believe that the way to real knowledge of the mystery of life lay in an understanding of one's own memories.

The early chapters of Muir's autobiography do not merely relate the things that happened to him. They describe a place and a way of life in terms of their significance to his understanding of human existence. Much of his poetry explores the same material.

Muir's readers have not missed these points. Almost all commentaries on his poems stress the significance to the poetry of the poet's experience, and particularly his experience of living in Orkney. Yet no published commentary has done more than generalize the nature of the experience, the result being that the connections between the poems and the early environment are merely asserted, not explained. The lack of information on the Orkney background as it really was is clearly an obstacle.

An even greater problem arising from the dependence on Muir's own writings for a knowledge of his background is a tendency among critics to avoid taking account of the obvious, but nevertheless crucial, distinction between biography and autobiography. When Muir's most important autobiographical work, *An Autobiography*, was reissued in 1980, Sheila Hearn, writing in *Books in Scotland*, broke new ground by questioning the unanimity and complacency of the critical reaction to its original publication and by complaining that criticism of Muir's writings appeared to have been frozen in a single stance for some forty years. She went on to suggest that critics of Muir's work, impressed by the obvious "sincerity" of *An Autobiography*, had failed even to consider that they might be reading a work of art, more than one of artlessness, and that Muir may have, in effect, been engaged in "setting up a totally self-reflexive system for the study of his work—a closed, exclusive world in which all his critics have been imprisoned."

One can recognize the truth of this statement without necessarily bringing into question the integrity and honesty that have been widely regarded as characteristic of *An Autobiography*. But to assert that the book is essentially a work of re-creation, and not a feat of memory, is to justify it as a work of art.

The early chapters of the autobiography reflect an experience which Muir himself considered crucial to him as a poet. This present study does not claim to improve on those chapters. What it seeks to do is to examine both the coherence of Muir's expression of that early experience in his poetry and prose, and to consider, through the study of contemporary reports and the recollections of others, the correspondence of that expression to the recorded actuality.

## Chapter One

# ORKNEY

ON SUMMER mornings the motor boat from Tingwall pushes its way through the stubby waves of Wyre Sound towards the little Orkney island of Wyre. On board are sacks of mail, a crate of milk, boxes of instant groceries, a bicycle or two, and a dozen or so tourists. The tourists clutch cameras and binoculars and stare at everything—at the wide horizon lined with dark islands, Rousay, Gairsay, Egilsay, Wyre itself; at the round tower of the church in Egilsay proclaiming the place where Earl Magnus met his saintly death; at the bobbing eider ducks and the swooping fulmars; at the grey seals lolling on the rocks at the Taing. Only the seals stare back.

On the left, part way up the hill in Rousay, stands the Victorian mansion of Trumland, built for his bride by a retired officer of the British Army in India. Opposite, on the summit of a little green mound in Wyre, is the relic of another empire. A century ago the local children believed that the broken tower of Cubbie Roo's Castle was once the home of a giant who enjoyed throwing rocks into the sea or at other islands. The tourists who climb up there today have the advantage of guide books which tell them that Cubbie Roo was not really a giant at all but only a Viking chieftain, Kolbein Hruga, who lived there early in the twelfth century.

Cubbie Roo's Castle has been measured and explained by the Department of the Environment and the tourists don't know about giants any more.

On the way to the Castle you pass a little farmhouse called the Bu. The tourists take photographs of it. It makes a point of interest in the foreground for anyone who wants a photograph of the great sweep of the Rousay hills. Few tourists know that the little huddle of farm buildings was once the home of Bjarni Kolbeinson, Son of Cubbie Roo himself, and a great Norse poet. Few know that eight hundred years later the Bu became the home

3

of another, perhaps greater, poet. Few know that around them lies
the raw material of that poet's work and that they are standing on
the isle where his childhood myth was enacted.

Things have changed since he lived there a century ago. The
pier, a white concrete finger pointing across the Sound, is a recent
gift from the Scottish Office. Across the water in Rousay most of
the old croft houses lie in ruins; and the stone dykes that march
across the hillside are crumbling. The eight farms of Wyre are
still occupied, but mainly by strangers. The old stories are no
longer told around the fireside on winter evenings; and the "soft
sing-song lilt of the islands, which has remained unchanged for
over a thousand years"[1] has given way before the incongruous
accents of Bootle and St John's Wood. The life of twelve
centuries, extending from the first Norse settlements to the
emigrations of the early twentieth century, has been broken. What
lives on is the unchanging landscape. And the poetry of Edwin
Muir.

It was at the age of two that Edwin Muir first set foot on Wyre.
He was born, on 15th May 1887, at a farm called the Folly on the
Mainland of Orkney. All that remains today of the house where
he was born is a line of stones, half hidden in the grass. Even its
name has disappeared from the map, for the lands are now joined
to a neighbouring farm. Muir was shown the ruins when he was a
man. He had no childhood memories of the place.[2]

In 1889 his father took the tenancy of the Bu in Wyre. The Bu,
with its 93 acres, was the largest farm in the island, and it was a
place with a long history: its very name indicates that it was once
the home of a local chieftain. James Muir was making his way in
the world. Or so he hoped.

Surprisingly, though perhaps fittingly, it was in Wyre that the
poet was baptised. He was then three years old and the ceremony
became his earliest memory.[3] It was one of many memories of his
childhood in Wyre that he came to cherish with unusual intensity.
But in a material sense the family did not make their way in Wyre
at all. The difficulty of finding the rent for an unsympathetic
landlord forced them in 1893 to a smaller farm on the island and
then to a farm on the Orkney Mainland. There Muir's father gave
up altogether the struggle to continue as a farmer. The family
moved briefly to Kirkwall, the county town, where Edwin had

already started school, before leaving Orkney for Glasgow in 1901.

Living in Glasgow proved a brutal and crucial experience. For Edwin it meant dispiriting work in a variety of offices; for his parents and two of his brothers it meant ill-health and an early grave. The contrast between the security and harmony of his life in Wyre and the suffering and break-up of his family in Glasgow was undoubtedly the central experience of the poet's life. It is recounted, vividly but without rancour, in his autobiography.

The autobiography is a remarkable work. The first version appeared in 1940 as *The Story and the Fable*. A revised and extended version was published in 1954 under the more prosaic title, *An Autobiography*. And he added an interesting postscript to the first version in the form of an article, "Yesterday's Mirror", in the *Scots Magazine* in September 1940. In this Muir considers not only the life he has led but the experience of writing about it. Writing his autobiography had convinced him that "our knowledge of life comes from yesterday, a yesterday which can never change again and is therefore beyond confusion." The belief about the role of the past informs much of Muir's poetry and criticism.

Critics generally have been very ready to recognize the importance of the autobiography. Reviewing *The Story and the Fable* on its publication in 1940, Stephen Spender thought it the most interesting book Edwin Muir had written and even went so far as to suggest, not too fancifully, that Muir had lived his life in order to write about it.[4] Herbert Read's review spoke of the book's "unique qualities of sincerity and beauty."[5] Q.D.Leavis, while lamenting that the book did not give the hoped-for account of the literary world following the first world war, called it "a wise book".[6] J.C.Hall maintained that the revised version, *An Autobiography*, "leads us to the very source of his inspiration and is indispensable to a full understanding of his work."[7] John Holloway expressed the view that *The Story and the Fable* "constitutes an almost unique document through which to see a poet's verse issuing from his life."[8]

Belief that the book is so important is tied up, not only with an appreciation of its intrinsic merits, but also with the assumption that Muir was a particular kind of poet. John Holloway expresses a fairly common view of Muir in suggesting that experience mattered so much to him because "the foundation of Muir's achievement as a poet is not a voguish manipulation of language, but the embodiment in verse of a true apprehension of life."[9]

The experience that Muir recounts in the later chapters of his autobiography are, on the face of it, those of a travelled man of the world. The course of his life took him to the industrial horrors of Glasgow immediately prior to the first world war, to literary London, to Austria and Czechoslovakia at a time when central Europe was simmering for another war, to Scotland again during the second world war, to Prague during the Communist coup of 1948, to the British Council in Rome, to the headship of an adult education college near Edinburgh, to America as a visiting professor, and to retirement near Cambridge. Yet no reader of his work can doubt that the six years spent in Wyre were what counted most or that it is the early chapters of *An Autobiography* that illumine Muir's poetry.

Butter regards the early chapters as "one of the most beautiful accounts of childhood ever written."[10] Christopher Wiseman says that the years spent in Wyre dominated the poet's entire life and provided the experience which "clearly sustains his powerful vision of Eden."[11] For Holloway the chapters on childhood form the best part of the book.[12] Muir's fellow Orcadian, fellow poet and friend, George Mackay Brown, in a broadcast in 1969, explains perhaps better than anyone has done, not only the importance to Muir of his early years, but also the importance of the act of remembering them for the composition of the autobiography:

> Before writing that book his past must have been pretty
> shapeless and dark and meaningless. In *The Story and the
> Fable*, by a pure cold act of memory, he found out what was
> really important in his life, that is, the innocence and the
> vision he had in his infancy in Orkney. He found that he still
> remembered it. He knew he must hold on to it, whatever
> happened.[13]

Writing his autobiography convinced Muir of the importance, not only to him, but to everyone, of holding on to the childhood vision. He saw the experience of childhood as much more than a useful source of material for a writer. "Yesterday's Mirror", written not long after the publication in 1940 of *The Story and the Fable*, outlines three ways in which men commonly look at their childhood. One man has forgotten his childhood: he is the realist who sees only a world where wrong triumphs. Another man has retained enough memory of childhood to let him see the rightness behind the apparent wrongness of things. The third man is the great poet or mystic who sees that both good and evil have their place: this mysterious and ultimate vision of life has much in common with the child's first perception of life. Muir recognizes that most people come into the second of these categories. His admirers might place him in the third.

He goes on to say that the realization of these three ways of looking at experience brought back to his mind a great number of forgotten impressions—the dignity of human beings, the separate dignity of old age and youth, the aptness of the animal world, the rightness of things made by human hands, the place of evil in the world.

One recognizes here some of the characteristic themes of his poetry. And the eye of childhood accounts also for the characteristic nature of his imagery. In an essay on the ballads Muir observes how the ballad makers use images as they are first seen in childhood—the simple vividness, for example, of silver, velvet and gold.[14] This is the kind of perception that makes much of Muir's imagery seem generalized and heraldic; and whether it is a weakness or a strength depends on one's point of view. It is decidedly unfashionable.

The importance of childhood perception undoubtedly also goes far to explain the role of dreams in Muir's poetry. Again, this aspect of his work is not to everyone's taste, but it is fundamental to the nature of his poetry. *An Autobiography* tells us that many of his memories came back to him in dreams, charged with a universal significance. Muir's feeling for childhood puts it on the border of immortality, and his interest in the "collective unconscious" suggests that he may have regarded some of the content of his dreams as arising, not from childhood experience as such, but from the inherited memories of the human race, Jung's "archetypes".

It is no doubt possible to argue that, while childhood is part of the essence of Muir, the fact that the childhood was in Orkney is only an accidental. Indeed the very title of the first version of his autobiography encourages the idea that Muir was more concerned with some eternal reality behind everyday events than with the events themselves. It might be that Orkney does not matter. Yet Muir makes it clear that both the story and the fable are important and that he would have them both:

> A man now, gone with time so long—
> My youth to myself grown fabulous
> As an old land's memories, a song
> To trouble or to pleasure us—
> I try to fit that world to this,
> The hidden to the visible play,
> Would have them both, would nothing miss.
>
> *Day and Night*

Muir distinguishes between the story and the fable, not to dismiss the story as a mere shadow thrown against a wall, not to say that the record of actual events is less significant than the mythical pattern that he discerned behind them, but rather to render both story and fable more full of meaning. He tries "to fit that world to this". The power of his best verse lies in the meeting of story and fable:

> My childhood all a myth
> Enacted in a distant isle;
> Time with his hourglass and his scythe
> Stood dreaming on the dial,
> And did not move the whole day long
> That immobility might save
> Continually the dying song,
> The flower, the falling wave.
>
> *The Myth*

This is not a recollection of immortality. Time may have been dreaming, but, for all that, the song still died and the wave fell. The child lived in innocence of the world, but the world moved. The myth is important, but so is the fact that it was "enacted in a distant isle". For the myth is not just an idea: it was "enacted" and it was "enacted" in a particular place. The place matters.

What is peculiar about the place is, in some respects, what is peculiar about Muir's story. It was agrarian; it had a continuous history of occupation extending back a thousand years; it had the remnants of a culture and an oral literature that had developed over those thousand years; it was still comparatively remote from the rest of the country; and it was small.

Muir remained faithful to this place, as George Mackay Brown bears witness:

> If I had to describe the islands to a stranger, their look and texture, I could say, "They're like the poems of Edwin Muir"—so faithful has Muir been to the visions and realities of his Orkney childhood. The very shapes of the islands on the water are like the calm lovely undulations of Muir's verse. The islands, like the poetry, have nothing in them terrible or spectacular; only the assurance of life going back to the pure unsullied sources of time.[15]

Muir's wife, Willa, discovered just how much Orkney meant to him. It took her a little while to do so. Having found that he was disappointed with living in Montrose in the years 1924-1926, she admitted later: "I did not yet understand that the secret compass pointing north in his breast really pointed to Orkney."[16]

As a young man living in Glasgow, Muir went every year to Orkney on holiday; and from time to time he toyed with the idea of settling there. He never came near putting such a scheme into effect, yet his letters to friends in Orkney betray a continual awareness of the "secret compass" in his breast. In 1937 a young Orkney writer, Ernest Marwick, sent some of his poems to Muir and asked for criticism and advice. The reply consisted of an honest and painstaking criticism of the poems, and Muir added: "I'm afraid I shan't get to Orkney this year, though I would like to."[17] Marwick became a close and lifelong friend. Later letters to him show Muir's homesickness:

> I should like to come to Orkney this year, but Willa is not yet fit for such a long journey. (19 July 1954)

> Stanley Cursiter invited us for lunch in Edinburgh yesterday ... He spoke of the unusually fine summer that Orkney is enjoying; I wish we could have shared it. (19 August 1955)

He did visit Orkney in the late summer of 1957. Ernest Marwick took him for a drive in the countryside near Kirkwall. As the sun set over Rousay Muir was quiet for a long time and then said, "Where, in all poetry, are the words for that?"[18]

Back in Cambridge, where he had now settled, he wrote to Marwick:

> The people around here are very nice, gentle and kind, both in Swaffam Prior and Cambridge. They remind me of Orkney. (24 December 1957)

> We often think of you both and of Orkney, and I often long to see it again. (24 June 1958)

> I would like to come up to Orkney next summer with Willa, if that is possible: I long to see it once more at least. (15 October 1958)

But Orkney did not see him again. In November 1958 he wrote to another Orkney poet, Robert Rendall, of "the homesickness which is never far from me when the associations of Orkney are involved. Happy those who never leave it."

He died on 3 January 1959 and is buried at Swaffam Prior.

## Chapter Two

# THE ISLAND

Weir Island is a small low lying island, not so large as Egil-shay. The soil is the same, and the culture very poor, and the crops unequal to what might be expected from proper man-agement. There is a ruinous church here, and a quire, but no steeple; and there is the vestiges of a fortification on a rising ground, a little from the place where the church stands. There is moss ground in a part of this island; and many seals are to be seen on the rocks at the west end of this island. The num-ber of the inhabitants is 65, the youngest child included.

So runs the Rev. James Leslie's account of the island of Wyre (or Weir, or Veira) in the "Old" Statistical Account of 1795-1798. Of the parish as a whole he writes: "This parish is composed of four islands, Rousay, Egilshay, Weir, and Inhallow, and two small holms or uninhabited islands. They are situated about three leagues north-west of the county town, Kirkwall, and lie cont-iguous to each other."

Half a century later, Mr Leslie's successor as minister of the parish, the Rev. George Ritchie, compiled his contribution to the "New" Statistical Account of 1842 by repeating Leslie's words almost without alteration. It seems that little had changed in fifty years.

For a less laconic account of that remote part of a remote island group in which Edwin Muir spent his boyhood one may turn to the report made by the Liberal Unionist candidate in the 1895 general election who visited the parish, evidently with some reluctance, in the year that the Muirs left it:

Rousay is like all the other islands in this belt or ring of islands. A big piece of rock, with high cliffs to the fierce Atlantic on the outer or western edge, rising into high, bare moorland hills in the centre, and sloping down to the sea in

11

poor, thin pasturage on the inner side. A few lean cattle were
discontentedly browsing; sheep were to be seen, white specks
on the hillside, wandering in search of blades of grass. A
rocky road wound grey over the brown hill, a low stone cot-
tage stood out here and there among the boulders on the
hillside; and there was not a tree to relieve the desolation.[1]

A visitor a decade earlier had turned a less jaundiced eye on the
scene: "To the south of Rousay a pretty green islet lies, like an
emerald in the sea. This delightful spot is Weir or Veira, the *Vigr*
of the Norsemen."[2]

The author of this romantic description was R. Menzies
Fergusson whose *Rambles in the Far North*, based on two visits to
Orkney in the summers of 1881 and 1882, ran into two editions.
One must remember, of course, that Fergusson's popular trave-
logue was, like several later such travelogues of Orkney, the fruit
of brief, easy-going and comfortable visits in fine weather; it is,
moreover, not always easy to distinguish in his book between
first-hand recording and hearsay. The Liberal Unionist candidate
is perhaps a more frank observer.

On the face of it Wyre would appear an unpromising nursery
for a young poet. The island is little more than a mile long and
less than a mile wide at its broadest part. The highest hill stands
104 feet above sea level. On the only other hill stands Cubbie
Roo's Castle, and this, together with the ruined chapel that stands
at the foot of the same hill, is probably the most interesting object
on the island. But the view is incomparable and the silence
unforgettable, and for Muir the island became a "fabled shore".

The richness of this environment lies in its very austerity, its
reduction of the world to what is elemental. It has, of course, the
attraction of being an island—an island, that is, that can be
comprehended as an island even by a small child. Frank and
Fritzie Manuel begin their comprehensive study, *Utopian
Thought in the Western World*, with a reminder that dreaming of
the "Blessed Isles" is found in all cultures. One might go further
and recognize in the island nature of so many literary and
traditional versions of Utopia not merely a geographical conven-
tion but a widespread belief that the clearly defined space of an
island is intrinsic to the very idea of Utopia. Sir Thomas More
had King Utopus order the inhabitants of Utopia to dig away the

causeway that connected their land to the rest of the world. It was
a symbolic act. Muir's island had no causeway connecting it with
the rest of the world; a poet brought up on such an island will
somehow be different from one brought up in Clapham or
Manchester. Stanley Cursiter, who was at school with Muir, has
suggested in a broadcast about the poet that the thing that is
different about an island is the sense of security it gives you—no
one can come upon you unawares.[3]

In the threat to that security, in the danger of invasion from
without, Muir found the theme for several poems. "The Town
Betrayed" evidently starts from such a situation. In "The Castle"
the course of invasion is itself the subject matter. The poem starts
with a statement of absolute security:

> All through the summer at ease we lay,
> And daily from the turret wall
> We watched the mowers in the hay
> And the enemy half a mile away.
> They seemed no threat to us at all.

What could the defenders have to fear? Their towering battle-
ments could not be taken by force. But treachery is always
possible:

> There was a little private gate,
> A little wicked wicker gate.
> The wizened warder let them through.

The wizened warder had, of course, been bribed:

> Our only enemy was gold,
> And we had no arms to fight it with.

Whether intended or not, the poem contains a blunt parable of the
Muir family's experience in Wyre, where gold was indeed their
only enemy, an enemy against which they were helpless. The
security which Stanley Cursiter recognized in that island fastness
evaporated before the economic helplessness of the family and the
demands of their landlord. Was General Frederick William Traill
Burroughs, who turned them out, the "wizened warder" of the

island? Physically he was certainly a very small man, but he wielded great economic power.

"The Good Town" shows less certainty about the cause of defeat. Disorder comes apparently from without, Muir suggests, but then perhaps it is some fault within ourselves that brought about the ruin of what was once a good town:

> How did it come?
> From outside, so it seemed, an endless source,
> Disorder inexhaustible. Yet sometimes now
> We ask ourselves, we the old citizens:
> "Could it have come from us? Was our peace peace?
> Our goodness goodness?"

No such doubts are to be found in the autobiography. If the disorder of adult life in the great world comes from both within and without, the disorder of childhood comes entirely from without. The impression that the autobiography gives of life in Orkney, and particularly of the years in Wyre, is one of great security, a security seen in retrospect as at least partly the result of the isolation of the place.

The growing boy would hardly have been aware of Wyre's isolation, but the experience of exile in Glasgow and later in London can only have drawn attention to the comforting remoteness of home from the rest of the threatening world. He wrote to Stephen Spender:

> I don't suppose you can have any idea how completely cut off Orkney was at that time: anyone who went down to Leith for a visit came back with news of a strange world.[4]

Yet this was only relatively true. The years immediately before Muir's birth had seen great improvements to communications between Orkney and the rest of the country. A correspondent who called himself "a visitor to Orkney" complained in a letter to the *Orcadian* in 1891 of the "miserable boat", which "rolled like a tub" and had sanitary arrangements "too bad to mention", that carried passengers from Thurso to Kirkwall.[5] But earlier arrangements had been worse. Samuel Laing recalled on his 81st birthday in 1893 that it had once taken him three weeks to get from Kirkwall to Leith.[6]

Generally tourists got no further than the county town and they found that quite exotic enough:

> The town itself is of foreign appearance—gables generally to the street. The streets are causewayed by an irregular pavement in the centre, and *abominably dirty*.[7]

> As we proceeded, the town seemed more and more foreign. Small courtyards shaded by trees—actual trees, thick with leaves—stood between the houses and the street. These houses, we were told, were the winter residences of wealthy Orcadians, in the days when steam and railways were unknown, and when consequently Edinburgh was as remote in the matter of time from Kirkwall as Paris now.[8]

Few of these visitors got as far as Wyre. The first inter-island steamer had carried out her maiden voyage in 1865 but, as Muir recalled, there was no pier on the island at that time and passengers had to be rowed out to the *Fawn* in a small boat. The few visitors that did come had to choose a day when the weather was fine. The journey to Kirkwall was considered too long and tiring for young Edwin to be allowed to take part in that great annual treat for island folk, a visit to the Lammas Market.[9]

The completeness of the island experience, and the poet's subsequent awareness of the remoteness that lay behind it, are likely to have played a crucial part in the way that Muir was to show locality in his poetry.

Muir in exile did not immediately develop any nostalgia for his native island. "For many years after leaving Wyre," he tells us, "I never dreamed about it once; it was as if that part of my life had been forgotten. My first dream of it came twenty-five years later, when I was being psychoanalysed in London."[10] And what he did dream on that occasion seems hardly nostalgic at all. He dreamed that he was reaching a place by boat; and what he says he saw is a series of images, many—though not all—of which can be related to the landscape of Wyre and Rousay—the milk-white sea and sky, a rim of a horizon, the tangle (seaweed) dripping from the pier, and above everything the great black mountain of Rousay. But the people there were strangers to him and, although he felt a great longing to return to the Bu, the dream ended before he could go in.

Later he dreamt of the Bu itself. It was surrounded by great trees with the thickest foliage he had ever seen. And over it was a low grey sky, a "particular sky" arching over it alone. Again, he did not go in.[11]

The awareness of the sky is very Orcadian. The round sky, which draws a horizon like an enclosing circle, is without doubt the strongest feature of the Orkney landscape. Of course, it is only over an island that one can have a "particular sky", one which you share with no one else. It is the sky, perhaps more even than the sea, that is the visual expression of isolation.

The analyst who unleashed these dreams, and who deserves some credit both for the poems that derive immediately from them and for the practice that Muir adopted of using the content of dreams as the material for poetry, was Maurice Nicoll. Nicoll was a pupil of Jung, and it seems clear that, apart from helping Muir to resolve his immediate emotional problems, he also passed on to the poet various Jungean theories which were of use to him in his handling of poetic material. Jung shows how it is possible for dream material to be used by the creative artist; he rejects the purely causalist approach to dreams and suggests that they contain more than repressed desires. Muir's poetic practice seems strongly influenced by this belief.

Most of the images in these dreams can be seen in terms of nostalgia, but the image of trees is a notable exception. The presence of trees is puzzling unless we assume that Muir was influenced in some way by folk memories of the Norse fascination with sacred and cosmic trees (of which the presence of a guardian tree, the rowan, alongside the older houses in Orkney is the only surviving sign). There were, and are, no trees in Rousay. We do know from Weld's account, quoted above, that there were trees in Kirkwall, the town in which Muir, somewhat unhappily, attended secondary school. Trees appear in several early poems, always, as in the prose account of the dream, to create an atmosphere of claustrophobia, often to denote treachery. The scene of "Betrayal" is a "wild wooden place" where the tree-trunks show "a front of silent treachery". A victim drowses "careless under the deadly tree" in "The Recurrence". "The City" ends in the horror of "our children in the deadly wood". The claustrophobic effect of

the wood is emphasised in "The Grove", in which there are no
fewer than three separate references to "the smothering grove".
The wood seems to represent a state of mind:

> You in imaginary fears
> Threading the terrors of a wood
> That has no place but in your mind.
>
> *Images*

At times it is associated with home:

> If I could
> I'd leap time's bound or turn and hide
> From time in my ancestral wood.
>
> *The Mountains*

Muir's nostalgia is here clouded both by uncertainty about the
future and fear that the past is beyond recovery. The ancestral
wood is a place where one can either hide or be trapped. At this
stage in his life Muir is uncertain whether he has escaped to some
kind of freedom or is in a permanent exile, an exile that he does
not know how to handle.

The nostalgia is coloured also by the knowledge that it was in
Paradise that he was doomed to exile. Even as he lay upon the
sunny hill, the grasses "threw straight shadows far away". He sees

> there within the womb,
> The cell of doom.
>
> *The Road*

In these early poems nostalgia is always tinged with dread. Even
his memory of the horses that pulled the plough in Wyre ends:

> Ah, now it fades! it fades! and I must pine
> Again for that dread country crystalline,
> Where the blank field and the still-standing tree
> Were bright and fearful presences to me.
>
> *Horses*

Perhaps the best demonstration of his conflicting feelings for Wyre in the period before the Second World War occurs in a poem that is not overtly about nostalgia at all, though the reference in it to "the bare wood below the blackening hill" is a pointer. "The Enchanted Knight" is about a knight, buried, helpless, but conscious. His situation is that of the one caught in a snare in "Betrayal" or, less obviously, that of the narrator in "The Mountains" who knows that "the days have closed" behind his back and who finds himself able neither to go forward nor return the way he came. An unwitting guide to "The Enchanted Knight" is to be found in a book by Muir's analyst, Maurice Nicoll, in which Nicoll draws on his experience in the First World War to describe shell-shock and to give it a wider reference.[12] He explains that when reality becomes formidable one's powers of extraversion are at first increased, but reality can assume such a terrible aspect that this normal reaction is engulfed in a totally different condition. Nicoll describes shell-shocked patients in military hospitals: "They lie in bed in a state of helplessness. This helplessness is of varying degree. They may be paralysed, blind, deaf or dumb, and this loss of function does not depend on local injury. ... They are incapable of any kind of effort."

The symbolism found in dreams was, Nicoll thought, likely to be significant in these cases. He instanced a shell-shocked patient who believed he was half-buried in earth, a symbol which Nicoll read as a sign of the patient's psychological condition and a partial return to the origins of life. Here we have an account of the very condition portrayed in the poem, itself an objectified account of Muir's own psychological state at the time he was treated by Nicoll. That Muir was himself quite well aware of his failure to adapt to a changed environment after his departure from Orkney is clear from his autobiography. The cultural shock that he suffered was akin to shell-shock.

Yet the early poems indicate that the regression to childhood was never more than partial. Just as in his dreams he avoided entering the Bu, so in "The Mountains" he reflects that there is no going back. Like the enchanted knight he is "rooted here" in the mountains; but the memory of his past is

> So far away, if I should turn
> I know I could not find

That place again.

Yet there does have to be a way forward. In a very fine poem,
"The Mythical Journey", he draws together several images from
his days in Wyre—the roofless chapel, Cubbie Roo's castle, the
black mountain of Rousay, and the beaches—and he sets them
behind him. He and his companions are on a voyage of discovery
to the great kingdom:

> How long ago? Then sailing up to summer
> Over the edge of the world. Black hill of water,
> Rivers of running gold. The sun! The sun!
> Then the free summer isles.
> But the ship hastened on and brought him to
> The towering walls of life and the great kingdom.

No commentator on this poem appears to have noticed that its
frame of reference is that of the voyage from Orkney to Jerusalem
and Constantinople early in the twelfth century by Rognvald
Kolson, Earl of Orkney, a voyage which is described in some
detail in the *Orkneyinga Saga* and which forms part of the
mythology of the Orkney people. There can be no doubt that
Muir would be familiar with the story of Rognvald Kolson's
voyage and little doubt that the poem refers to it. The "great
kingdom" is obviously Jerusalem, in both its earthly and heavenly
forms, and the "towering walls of life" may well refer to the walls
of Constantinople guarded by Rognvald's compatriots, the Varan-
gians. The reference in the Saga to the death of many of
Rognvald's companions in the Holy Land, the traditional myth
that Adam lies buried at Golgotha and that this was the starting
point of creation as well as the point of redemption, and the age-
old symbols of the Mountain and the Tree of Life (both indicative
of the centre of the world and the point of creation) are all drawn
together in the image of

> the dead scattered
> Like fallen stars, clustered like leaves hanging
> From the sad boughs of the mountainous tree of Adam
> Planted far down in Eden.

"The Mythical Journey" is an early example in Muir's work of the tendency, found in many traditional societies and described by Mercea Eliade in *The Myth of the Eternal Return*, to conceive of contemporary events as repetitions of archetypal behaviour. Here we may say that Muir is converting his own experience of exile into what Eliade calls a "paradigmatic gesture", a repetition of the act of a mythical hero drawn from the past of his own society. Exile has to be made bearable, and one way to make it bearable is to see it as the repetition of an archetypal act. Such gestures became a feature of Muir's work; and for the sources of the mythical events which he used to transfigure his own experience he turned to Greek mythology, the Bible, traditional ballads, and German and English literature. The gesture here belongs entirely to Orkney.

The island has some responsibility too for Muir's particularly strong, and characteristic, sense of place. Of the volumes of his verse, the titles of all but two refer to places; every one of the chapters of his autobiography is the name of a place; and one can open at random the volume of his collected poems many times before one can find a poem in which the locus of the events is not strongly asserted.

Muir generally is not a descriptive poet. His landscape, however vivid its effect on the reader, is a semi-abstraction in the manner of Expressionist painting, in which the image moves a step nearer to the idea than one finds in representational art. One looks in vain for an Orkney equivalent of Wordsworth's Lake District or Hardy's Wessex. In Wordsworth and in Hardy the landscape is an essential presence. In Muir it is something different again: it is a space marked out from the rest of the world, a space defined as an arena for the particular action. It is not so much described as identified and delineated:

> Here at my earthly station.
>
> *The Stationary Journey*

> This is the place.
>
> *The Threefold Place*

> The angel and the girl are met.

Earth was the only meeting place.

*The Annunciation*

It is the perspective of an islander to comprehend the limits round him and see his land as a whole. Muir's drawing of boundaries serves to isolate the place of the action and thereby intensify the reader's awareness of both the uniqueness and the universality of what is happening there. Like King Utopus, Muir creates islands. They are not always surrounded by water in the literal sense, but they are islands for all that.

Not only are Muir's landscapes firmly delineated, but they are also, without being systematically described, firmly characterized. They have the common characteristic of setting the rest of the world at a distance, reflecting the emptiness and the wide horizons of the Orkney landscape that Muir remembered. The view from Wyre was not a desolate one. Muir's memory registered for ever the soft colours and the isolated features of the tower of the old church in Egilshay, the castle in Wyre, the black mountain of Rousay, and the low hills separated by narrow stretches of water that lay everywhere around. It was a Wyre landscape more specifically than it was an Orkney landscape. Muir found the view from the farm of Garth, near Kirkwall, to which the family moved from Wyre in 1895, disappointing, though as the crow flies it was only a few miles from Wyre: "The landscape was rough and desolate, the landscape of a second-rate saga; it did not have the beautiful soft colours of Wyre and the islands round; the red island of Eday, the dark green island of Egilshay with its tower, the blue-black hills of Rousay."[13] The very simplicity of such a landscape seems to have made it an inspiration to the poet; we find its few sparse features used again and again in the poems.

Muir's practice suggests a fascination with the possibilities of moving the same few features around in the landscape to produce a virtually endless series of variations. In his autobiographical novel, *Poor Tom*, the character who most resembles Muir himself, Mansie, asks himself: "Why was one thing in one place and another in another? A complete riddle the way things were scattered about on the face of the earth, hills and houses and rocks and gates and horses." Such features are moved around in Muir's verse and placed here and there, not so much as a way of

describing the scene through the selection of detail as rather a
kind of symbolic and emotional shorthand. He does not attempt a
graphic description of the scene: he uses images to evoke emotion.

As an example we might take the occasional evocation of the
little green hills of Wyre. Muir was at first unconscious of the
effect of these hills on him, and congratulated Alec Aitken who
had spotted the connection between the "little hills" of "The
Mythical Journey" and the poet's recognition that a dream of "a
great plain dotted with little conical hills", recounted in *An
Autobiography*,[14] referred to the little hills of his childhood. "I
have been pursued by these little hills often without quite
knowing where they came from," he wrote to Aitken. "I realized
when I wrote the autobiography."[15]

The little hills appear again in "Holderlin's Journey":

> At noon I came
> Into a maze of little hills,
> Head-high and every hill the same.
> A little world of emerald hills.

That they are "emerald" rather than the soft green of Orkney,
that they form a tight mass within a little world that conveys more
the claustrophobic fears than the happy innocence of childhood,
tells us something of the feverish state of Holderlin's mind as he
journeys in search of the woman he has lost. Mansie had
wondered why things were in one place rather than another;
Holderlin, hovering between sanity and madness, sees a landscape
dissolving and re-arranging itself:

> The hills and towers
> Stood otherwise than they should stand,
> And without fear the lawless roads
> Ran through all the land.

"Holderlin's Journey" demonstrates that Muir turned to Orkney
for symbols of terror and frustration as well as for those of
consolation and harmony. A comparison of this poem with "The
Labyrinth" shows also how the same symbols can be used to quite
different effect.

The formal structure of "The Labyrinth" merges the poet's experience with that of Theseus seeking the Minotaur; it is another example of Muir's tendency to explain his own less pleasant experiences in terms of archetypal actions. The urban terrors of Glasgow had had a powerful effect on the teenager from Orkney who had never seen a train, a tram, a factory, or a tenement. He turned his innocent eye to good account. Muir can convey the unreal, sinister connotations of the industrial landscape in a way that sheer familiarity with it makes impossible for other poets of his time. He sees urban surroundings, not merely as the neutral environment of one's daily affairs, but as an actual landscape. Where a townsman is moved by the sunset in a Highland glen, the boy from Wyre is moved, though in a different way, by his first sight of the Canongate in Edinburgh: "Perhaps it is the height of the houses, the great number and smallness of the windows, and the narrowness of the space in which one has to walk that gives this sense of watchfulness and sinister familiarity. But there is in it, too, something of the terror of narrow rocky passes in savage and possibly inhabited regions."[16] A similar response is found in Hans, the half-witted, or innocent, boy in Muir's novel, *The Marionette*. Hans has seldom been allowed to leave his house to visit the nearby town of Salzburg. When he does venture into the town he is frightened by the buildings: "Hans looked up at the houses towering above him; they seemed to be toppling at every moment; they would fall on him."[17]

The sense that so many people are living around one, the lack of privacy, the feeling that one is being watched by strangers, the sheer physical quantity of the human contribution to the landscape, is frightening. In Glasgow Muir walked to work every day through the slums. He learned eventually the defence of familiarity. He became a townsman who did not see the horror, but "if I was tired or ill I often had the feeling, passing through Eglinton Street or Crown Street, that I was dangerously close to the ground, deep down in a place from which I might never be able to climb up again."[18] This was the labyrinth. It became a major image in Muir's poetry. Its origins lie in Muir's first experience of urban landscape and its contrast with the open landscape of the island.

It is in the title poem of the 1949 collection, *The Labyrinth*, that the image finds its fullest development in Muir's work. The labyrinth in which the poet finds himself is not some special place, but the whole noisy world itself. And it is an urban world of treacherous streets:

> There have been times when I have heard my footsteps
> Still echoing in the maze, and all the roads
> That run through the noisy world, deceiving streets
> That meet and part and meet.

This urban labyrinth contrasts with the natural world:

> the still fields swift with flowers, the trees
> All bright with blossom, the little green hills, the sea,
> The sky and all in movement under it.

Which of these worlds is the real one? It was easy for the young boy from Wyre to be persuaded that the world of Glasgow, of slums, of industry and commerce, and all the attitudes that go with it, was the real world. The people who inhabit that world do not see Wyre as belonging to the real world at all: it is only Utopia. But Muir's security as an individual depended ultimately on his being assured that Wyre was indeed of the real world and that the other world was a lie. Securing this conviction, through the recognition of what is fine in the archetypal patterns and the way they relate to the poet's own experience, is the preoccupation of much of his poetry, and never more positively so than here in "The Labyrinth". The fear of being trapped for ever "deep in the centre of the endless maze" must be overcome by the memory of the little green hills; and the poet is in a position to claim that there is indeed another world:

> For once in a dream or trance I saw the gods
> Each sitting on the top of his mountain-isle,
> While down below the little ships sailed by,
> Toy multitudes swarmed in the harbours, shepherds drove
> Their tiny flocks to the pastures, marriage feasts
> Went on below, small birthdays and holidays,
> Ploughing and harvesting and life and death,
> And all permissible, all acceptable.

"There are," wrote George Mackay Brown, commenting on this part of the poem, "many places in Orkney where one can find this deep indescribable peace and security,"[19] Clearly the scene does have an Orkney genesis, though it is filtered through dream. Dream both distances the memory and gives it immediacy:

> That was the real world; I have touched it once,
> And now shall know it always.

These two lines are perhaps the most direct assertion in all Muir's verse of the continuing reality and presence of the world he knew in his early years. The conviction helps him escape

> the lie,
> The maze, the wild-wood waste of falsehood, roads
> That run and run and never reach an end.

None of this seems to have had much to do with the story of Theseus and the Minotaur. Yet it would be a mistake to assume that the traditional Greek myth was no more than a convenience for Muir, allowing him to contrast the worlds of his boyhood and his manhood. The poem is more complex than such a simple antithesis would suggest, and the myth itself is more complex than most of us know it.

For a history of the idea of the labyrinth one can turn to an essay by C.M. Deedes, published in a collection of essays on myth and ritual edited by S. H. Hooke.[20] Deedes traces the spread of labyrinth building from Egypt, to Crete and Athens, to Troy, and from Troy, via trade routes to Scandinavia, where labyrinths have been discovered on islands in the Baltic, in Finland, Sweden, Norway and Iceland. He identifies the stone circles of Britain, among which there are two fine examples in Orkney, with the labyrinth tradition. He demonstrates that the purpose of the original labyrinths in Egypt could not have been to confuse potential robbers of the royal tomb that lay at the centre. The labyrinths of Egypt were the architectural and symbolic setting for a sacred drama of life and death, in which the old king-god (or later, the bull substitute) was sacrificed to make way for the new. When a time came that the king was not sacrificed in person, he still sought the centre of the labyrinth each year, to return, after a symbolic death, reborn. The heart of the labyrinth is then a symbol of creation, or rebirth as well as death.

If the cult was widespread in Scandinavia, it would be surprising if it did not have a lasting effect on the unconscious symbolism of the northern mind. Muir did more than use this myth as a framework for biography. He moved, through unconscious symbolism, to the very heart of the myth. The modern reader tends to think that the important aspect of the Theseus story is the theme of escape. And there is an element of the escape story in the poem. But set in tension with it is the theme of the older myth of reaching the heart of the labyrinth and thereby gaining renewed life. The clues to the motif of rebirth ("bloodsplashed", "dead or alive") are clearly pointed. The vision of the gods, while it is the antithesis of the vision of the labyrinth, is available only to those who go into the labyrinth. In biographical terms one may say that Muir was able to understand and idealize the world of Orkney only because he came to have experience of a world he could not idealize. The labyrinth is the experience of exile.

In "The Labyrinth" the word "road" (or "roads") occurs no fewer than twenty-four times. The road is a symbol that appears again and again in Muir's poetry. He wrote, at different times, two quite separate poems called "The Road". This preoccupation with the road symbol is curious. He can have known few roads when he was a child. At one point in his autobiography he claims that there were no roads in Wyre at that time.[21] Yet in the previous chapter of the same book, in the course of describing a childhood fight, he remembers that "the other boy, whose name was Freddie, was standing with me at a place where two narrow roads crossed."[22] His memory must have been at fault at one of these points, unless he is making a distinction, unconvincing in an Orkney context, between "roads" and "narrow roads". It is most unlikely that he is making any such distinction, but he may have been led into inconsistency by an unconscious memory of an earlier encounter between Oedipus and a stranger

> at that predestined point
> Where three paths like three fates crossed one another.
> *Oedipus*

His instinct was to assuage the shame of the memory by relating it
to a mythical event; his encounter with Freddie Sinclair is
transformed into Greek myth in the poem, "Ballad of Hector in
Hades". His memory is, in any case, likely to be confused on this
point because it was while he was actually living in Wyre as a
child that the first road was made there. The Orkney Roads Act
came into force in 1857 and the provision of roads began with a
road between Kirkwall and Stromness. By June 1893 the demand
for roads had reached the smaller islands; Orkney County Council, using a special government grant supplied for building roads
to schools, responded to a suggestion from Rousay School Board
and built a road along the ridge in the centre of Wyre to connect
the school with the farms.

Whatever Muir's memory made of it, the building of the road
in Wyre must have been an event much talked of in his boyhood
and it left an impression on his imagination which, in poem after
poem, suggested roads as a key symbol. He detected the same
symbol in Kafka:

> The image of a road comes into our minds when we think of
> his stories; for in spite of all the confusions and contradictions
> in which he was involved he held that life was a way, not a
> chaos, that the right way exists and can be found by a sup-
> reme and exhausting effort.[23]

What is true here of Kafka is also true of Muir. For him the right
way exists and can be found. Muir uses the road symbol in quite a
complex way, to provide a whole range of images, and more often
to raise a question than to state a position. The road is the symbol
both of the inevitability of exile and the possibility of returning
from it, the symbol both of the search for knowledge of one's own
soul and the treachery and deceit of the world around that make
that knowledge difficult to attain, the symbol both of the
individual's right to choose and the accidents of fate that negate
choice.

Life offers possibilities of action which the adventurous soul
should seize. He should learn

> the paths to know
> That thread the labyrinthine park,

And the great Roman roads that go
Striding across the untrodden day.

*Day and Night*

The opportunities may be deceptive:

The confident roads that at their ease beguile me
With the all-promising lands, the great unknown,
Can with their gilded dust blind me, defile me.

*My Own*

The protagonists of "The City" (Rognvald's crusaders again?)
who

kept the dusty road,
And nearer came small-towered Jerusalem,

were the victims of self-deception. They had

dared
Half the world's spite to hit the mark of bliss.

But what they found at the end was a dead land and the memory
of

The streets of the holy city running with blood,
And the centuries of fear and power and awe,
And all our children in the deadly wood.

Here the dusty road symbolizes the path of self-deception and
eventual fearful understanding of the reality of ideals in this
world. But the road can symbolize also the deceits of others, as in
"The Escape":

The endless trap lay everywhere,
And all the roads ran in a maze
Hither and thither, like a web
To catch the careless days.

Or in "The Three Mirrors":

> The hunting roads ran on
> To round the flying hill
> And bring the quarry home.

The difficult journey (for example, the Crusades, the search for the Golden Fleece) is, according to Eliade, a universal symbol of the search for the centre, for the point of creation, for the understanding of the inner self, for absolute reality. The road and the labyrinth are examples of this symbol.[24] Muir uses the symbol invariably in the sense postulated by Eliade. His search for absolute reality, which led him in the end to a very personal form of Christianity, cannot be contained in a simple framework of his physical and emotional exile from Orkney, but that exile did relate to a myth through which he could seek an understanding of his search. The landscape of the myth is the landscape of Wyre.

Chapter Three

# FAMILY

Seek the beginnings, learn from whence you came
And know the various earth of which you are made.

*The Journey Back*

MUIR HAD a strong sense of identification with his forebears; it
was a feeling he thought important for men in general; yet he was
oddly incurious about his actual genealogy. He confessed that he
knew no details of any ancestors beyond his grandparents on both
sides: his father's parents had lived at the farm of Colligarth in
Sanday and his mother's at the farm of Skaill in Deerness on the
mainland of Orkney. He mentions in *An Autobiography* that the
island of Sanday is full of Muirs who had come from Scotland to
Orkney at the beginning of the sixteenth century in the wake of
the Stewart earls.[1] Muir's preference for the emotional security of
a general ancestral awareness to the historical trivia of the family
tree is characteristic of the perception of traditional societies,
where the past is seen more as a timeless repetition of archetypes
than as a linear sequence of individuals and events. It is the
modern urban man who is often most anxious to research the bare
details of names and dates of his own particular forebears. For
Muir, what matters is not the decorative but irrelevant family
tree—irrelevant because it teaches him no lessons about his own
life—but the sense of the forebears of the tribe living in him:

> Unless in me my father live
> I can never show
> I am myself—ignorant if
> I'm a ghost or no.

*Twice-Done, Once-Done*

> Then suddenly again I watch the old
> Worn saga write across my years and find,
> Scene after scene, the tale my fathers told.

*Too Much*

Imagination tells us that we become human by repetition,
that our life is a rehearsal of lives that have been lived over
and over.

*Essays in Literature and Society,* 225

When he says that the Muirs first came to Orkney with the
Stewart earls in the sixteenth century Muir is actually understat-
ing the time of their arrival by two centuries. In the records of the
earldom collected by Clouston (1914) one Adam of Mwre is listed
in a document dated 25 May 1369 as one of the Scots followers of
the Bishop of Orkney. Thome of Muyr is listed among the leading
men giving judgment regarding an inheritance in June 1516; on
the reverse of this document is the statement that it is "the dome
of the best landit men and royht men in Orkna at that time."

So the Muirs were Scots, not Norse, and it seems that they
settled first in the neighbourhood of Kirkwall where the bishop
had his palace and cathedral; later they moved to the island of
Sanday and were listed among the principal proprietors there in
1501.[2] There they remained, the poet's father himself being born
in Sanday. But their wealth and importance diminished. They
became one of the many Orkney families that fell in the social
scale as wealth and power were concentrated in fewer hands in the
centuries following the rule of the Stewart earls. In 1812 there
were 218 landowners in Orkney and not a Muir among them.[3] Yet
the number of families bearing the name had increased tremen-
dously. A survey taken in 1887, the year of the poet's birth, shows
that there were 505 families called Muir, heavily concentrated in
Sanday and its neighbouring island of North Ronaldsay, and that
the name was then the seventh most common in Orkney.[4]

His mother's family name, Cormack, gets not one mention in
any of the ancient records collected by Clouston, but it is a well-
established name in Orkney, and Edwin Muir liked to think that
there was a connection with a Saint Cormack who, in the eight or
ninth century, built a chapel in Deerness near to the place where
Muir's mother was born.[5] Whatever the truth of this story, it
seems certain that Muir's ancestors on both sides had lived in a
small area and had a mixture of Scots, Norse and Celtic blood in
them. Muir was aware of this mingling—in a letter to T.S.Eliot he
says that the Orkney people "are a mixture of everything"[6]—but,

in common with most of his countrymen, he liked to stress the Norse, as against the Scots, kinship. The Scots, who acquired the islands from Denmark in 1468, were popularly seen as oppressors and exploiters. The days of Norwegian sovereignty, which had preceded those of the Danish, and the widespread ownership of land which was supposed to have constituted the odal system, a system supplanted by feudalism only after the annexation by Scotland, were fondly remembered, even in the nineteenth century, as some kind of Golden Age.

Although Muir wrote a good deal on Scotland and the Scots, he rejected Scottish nationalism as "a trivial response to a serious problem."[7] He explained to his brother-in-law, "After all, I'm not Scotch, I'm an Orkney man, a good Scandinavian, and my true country is Norway, or Denmark, or Iceland, or some place like that. But this is nonsense, I'm afraid, though there's some sense in it, as Lizzie will agree."[8] There is something tentative, even shame-faced, about this statement. Muir's assertion of his cultural heritage cannot be expressed without including both "nonsense" and "some sense". The modern Orkney man has been Scotticised and Anglicised to an extent that confuses him; but, if he is at all culturally sensitive, he cannot escape some nostalgia for his Scandinavian past. Muir felt this nostalgia strongly enough to repeat the folk tradition that the Orkney people came originally from two valleys in southern Norway.[9]

Outsiders saw both the nostalgia and the reasons for it. Christian Ployen, a Danish visitor to Kirkwall in 1839, was assured on every hand that, being a Dane, he was not a foreigner but a compatriot, and he observed how often the question was discussed as to whether the annexation of Orkney by Scotland was irrevocable.[10] A Norwegian visitor, entering an Orkney house in 1849, was so struck by the Norse appearance of the children that he was surprised to hear them speak English.[11]

A sensitive insider, George Mackay Brown, sees the Norse period as Orkney's Golden Age: "There is no doubt that the heroic Norse period was the most splendid that Orkney ever knew. Great men walked in the islands. Orkney had need of its heroic age, because soon there was to come a time of bitterness and degradation."[12]

The Stewart earls, for all that they built a splendid Renaissance palace in Kirkwall, were remembered for having brought squalor

and neglect to the islands. The squalor and neglect continued
almost until our own time. The standard of housing, for example,
remained low until the second half of the nineteenth century
when landlords started to undertake the construction and repair
of their tenants' houses. In Wyre the factor, Robert Scarth, had
improved all the houses before the Muir family moved there.[13] In
1891 their landlord wrote:

> The people of Orkney are not Celts. The clan system never
> existed here. They were well fed, well clothed, well housed,
> and well off. ... Want and misery are here simply unknown.[14]

General Burroughs was, of course, hardly an unbiassed observer,
and he is clearly exaggerating the prosperity and happiness of his
tenants; but that there was some truth in his statement is
confirmed by the memories of a more obviously objective witness,
John Wilson, who was appointed assistant school inspector for
Orkney in 1889 and, as such, travelled widely on behalf of the
government in Orkney and elsewhere:

> In those days the contrast between the conditions in the
> Hebrides and the Orkney Islands was remarkable. In the
> former one was struck by the comparative poverty of the bulk
> of the people, whereas in the latter the prevailing tone was
> comfort and contentment.[15]

It is confirmed also by figures published in 1892 which show that
the ratio of paupers to the population generally was in Orkney
greater than in ten other Scottish counties but less than in twenty-
two.[16] Hunger had become more of a memory than a threat.
Contemporaries of Muir told Ernest Marwick of the tradition,
still well known in their youth, that in times of famine people
collected "ebb meat" (shell fish) from the shore.[17] For them the
story had already the quality of legend.

The diet of the Muir family described in *An Autobiography* [18]
appears adequate if monotonous—herring, potatoes, porridge,
crab, plovers' eggs, milk, butter and cheese. But the poet did once
confess to his wife that the only kind of cooking his mother knew
was boiling everything, and Willa suspected that her husband's
small bones were the result of deficiencies in his diet as a boy.[19]

Nowhere in *An Autobiography* or anywhere else in Muir's works does there appear the slightest complaint about the physical conditions in which he was brought up. On the contrary, life at the Bu is pictured as one of the greatest contentment. Some of his poems suggest even analogies between his own family and the Holy Family of Nazareth. The opening lines of "Childhood" echo the phrase in St John's Gospel, "In my father's house there are many mansions":

> Long time he lay upon the sunny hill,
> To his father's house below securely bound.

At the end of section six of "The Journey Back", a poem which explores the possibility of return to man's origins, the line

> Here on this road, following a falling star

evokes the memory of the Magi seeking the home of the Holy Family. The same image appears in "The Sufficient Place":

> See, all the silver roads wind in, lead in
> To this still place like evening. See, they come
> Like messengers bearing gifts to this little house,
> And this great hill worn down to a patient mound.

Here the poet returns, in imagination, to his home. The "silver roads" may be a reminder of one of the gifts of the Magi, may refer also to the stretches of water one must cross to get to Wyre. The hill, which seemed great when the poet was a child, is now worn down by the effects of time and experience: it has become one of the "little hills".

One need not be surprised by the analogy with the Holy Family. It is an accessible archetype. In this poem it is an archetype that Muir points to quite consciously:

> This is the Pattern, there the Archetypes,
> Sufficient, strong and peaceful.

As a child he saw his parents as "fixed allegorical figures in a timeless landscape"; and he makes the point that while most men

and women are secondary images because we know them first as
strangers, our parents are never unknown, never strangers.[20]

A late notebook entry shows how the implied association with
the Holy Family never faded:

> About my father and mother
> Realising long after their death their virtue and
> goodness
> How could they have been what they were but for
> Incarnation
> The incarnation of a soul in a body
> Simplicity, grace, infinite patience and kindness.[21]

The four nouns in the last line of this draft carry the essence of
the description of his parents in the autobiography. What stands
out in that description is the lack of aggression in the household.
They were not a quarrelsome family; unusually for the time, his
father never struck him. When, years after his father's death,
Muir heard an old friend, John Ritch, describe "Cheems Muir" as
an "inoffensive man", it seemed to him the highest praise that
could be given to anyone. James Muir was, in that respect, typical
of his race and upbringing. Orkney men were not noted for their
aggression: their known dislike of physical violence was one of the
reasons that the Hudson's Bay Company made a practice,
throughout the nineteenth century, of recruiting large numbers of
Orkneymen. Aggression may have served a useful social purpose
in the clan system of the Scottish Highlands, but it was of no
value in the settled, agrarian, and isolated society of the Orkney
Islands.

Yet James Muir could not have been without drive and some
kind of ambition. He was born in the island of Sanday at the farm
of Colligarth which had been farmed by Edward Muir, his father,
and John Muir, his grandfather. It was no mere croft: it consisted
of 127 acres and employed in James' youth a number of labourers.
The 1861 census return shows him, at the age of 29, a self-
employed farmer and head of a family that consisted of his
widowed mother, his unmarried elder brother, two sisters, two
nephews and a domestic servant. The elder brother is described as
"farm labourer" and one can only speculate as to why James
should have assumed the leadership.

The agricultural depression of the last quarter of the nineteenth century made it inevitable that James Muir should have had difficulty in surviving as a farmer. But for a long time he did survive, moving from Colligarth to four other farms in various parts of Orkney before giving up farming altogether and moving south. In this downward spiral he clung to the land for as long as he could; unlike many of his class he never became a landless labourer. Even his move to Glasgow in 1905, disastrous to the health and happiness of his family as it proved to be, was a positive and bold move. He was no passive victim.

James was, moreover, a man whose intelligence was recognized by his neighbours. William Stove, who knew him well, described him to Ernest Marwick in 1971:

> He had broon hair an' a sma' beard. He wis pale an' niir tek on the sun. His neck wis twisted tae the wan side. He could be very quiet, bit if he kent you he could spaek fine. Sometimes he wad spaek a lot, an' spaek to some purpose, for he wis a clivir man.[22]

The extended family of which James Muir was head was also the working and economic unit of the farm, a concept which hardly applies today even in agricultural communities in Britain. At the time of the 1841 census there were twelve people living at Colligarth, ranging in age from James's grandfather, who was then eighty, to james himself, aged nine. The 1851 return lists ten occupants, including two servants aged twelve and fifteen. In 1861 there were eight people in the house, including two young nephews and a female domestic servant. In Wyre the family at the Bu had ten members at the time of the 1891 census. These were James and his wife; their children, James, William, John, Lizzie, Clara and Edwin; James's unmarried sister, Margaret; and his nephew, William Sutherland.

Both his aunt Margaret and his cousin William made distinctive contributions to Edwin's education. Both were characters drawn rather larger than life. Maggie—at least, in the eyes of her nephews and nieces—was distinctly odd; she believed, for example, in a range of folk-superstitions and medico-superstitious remedies for her many ailments.[23] Sutherland was, for his cousin, a marvellous example of vigorous life—a drinker, chaser of girls, and inventor of facts, stories and even words.[24] He appears, without even his name being disguised, in *The Three Brothers*, and he is the subject of that thoughtful and affectionate late poem, "There's Nothing Here". According to this poem, what is wrong with heaven, from Sutherland's point of view, is that it lacks the ordinary pleasures of the earth—the feel of the plough's stilts and the horses' reins, the smell of peat and dung and cattle. These are not the intellectual and artistic pleasures valued by his cousin, the poet; but Muir's membership of that large family in Wyre enables him to appreciate from the inside the pleasures of the others.

But among the network of relationships at the Bu, that which mattered most was the relationship with his father. This is clear, not only in the autobiography, but in the presence of his father, and the implied importance of the father-son relationship, in two of his early novels, *The Three Brothers* and *The Marionette*.

John Blackadder, the father in *The Three Brothers*, is far from being a merely inoffensive man. Muir seems to go out of his way to stress Blackadder's ability and authority. This man of the Renaissance had travelled in France and Germany, had a wide knowledge of literature, had educated his son at home and taught him to overcome "all the secret terrors that had oppressed him". This is an idealized portrait of James Muir, the simple farmer from Colligarth. That his son should have wished to idealize him suggests the importance of their relationship and the depth of his admiration for his father.

*The Marionette* also is dominated by a father-son relationship, though it is the least autobiographical and, perhaps for that reason, the most successful of Muir's three novels. Hans is a "feeble-minded" boy who, since the death of his mother, has spent much of his time sitting in silence in his room at the top of the house, cared for by the housekeeper and avoided by his father. A totally new life starts for the child when his father starts to take an interest in him. It is the father who shows the outside world, the father who, by giving him a marionette, frees his imagination.

In both these novels the father is the source of strength and power. James Muir's mildness of manner, his failure as a farmer, his economic weakness in the face of a grasping landlord, his inability to put down roots in the strange land that was industrial Glasgow, do not make him a weakling. The clear eyes of the poet know that the archetypes of his home are

Sufficient, strong and peaceful.

*The Sufficient Place*

Muir's determination to cling to the memory of those early years in Wyre is partly to be explained by the poignancy of the eventual break-up of the family. The break-up came with dramatic suddenness after their move to Glasgow. As a teenager Muir saw his father die of a heart attack. Within four years of his father's death two of his brothers died, Willie of consumption, Johnnie of a tumour on the brain; and within a few months of Johnnie's death their mother also had died.

Years later Muir recorded these events, carefully, without overstatement, yet painfully:

> The family now looked as if it had been swept by a gale. Only four were left: my two sisters, Jimmie and myself; and as we were grown up—I was eighteen—we presently went our own ways.[25]

The last phrase is particularly striking: because Edwin, the youngest, was now eighteen, they went their separate ways. They were never close again. Willa Muir was struck by the remoteness of their manner to one another.[26]

Except in that one phrase—"we presently went our own ways"—there is no hint anywhere in the autobiography of any dissension in the family or of any reason for the break-up of the family other than illness and death. Yet it is a curious fact that dissensions between members of a family constitute an element in all three of his novels; in two of them, *Poor Tom* and *The Three Brothers*, these dissensions take the form of bitter quarrels between brothers. In *Poor Tom* the brothers, divided over a girl, do not speak to one another. And their mother believes in her heart that their division is a consequence of their exile. Living in Glasgow is not merely unpleasant, it corrupts family relationships. Their troubles were "the portion of the corruption of Glasgow allotted to them, their private share of the corruption that was visible in the troubled, dirty atmosphere, the filth and confusion of the streets, the cynical frankness, hitherto unknown to her, with which people here talked of their privatest affairs, their fathers and mothers, sisters and brothers."[27]

Mrs Manson's belief that the place itself corrupted the family, that it allotted to them a private share of the great public corruption, relates to the theme of the third chapter of the autobiography, but it goes much further. The autobiography describes squalor and misfortune, but not the inner corruption of individuals. Is the inner corruption portrayed in *Poor Tom* simply an element in the fiction? Or is it something that Muir can talk about only under the guise of fiction?

By the time that he came to write the poem "The Brothers", many years after *Poor Tom*, Muir was able to face the death of his brothers with greater equanimity:

> Last night I watched my brothers play,
> The gentle and the reckless one.

The pain has been assuaged by time, by the transfiguration of the memory in dreams, and by the adoption of a traditional literary form. A much earlier poem, in which Muir openly uses the style of the Scottish ballad, begins in a very similar way:

> "Last night I dreamed a ghastly dream
> Before the dirl o' day."
>
> *Ballad of the Flood*

In "The Brothers" Muir reflects the form without simply imitating it.

The young man who wrote *Poor Tom* expressed through the mouth of Mrs Manson the thought that it was life in one particular place, Glasgow, that destroyed family relationships. The more mature poet of "The Brothers" knows that evil is not peculiar to Glasgow:

> I have observed in foolish awe
> The dateless mid-days of the law
> And seen indifferent justice done
> By everyone on everyone.

Human relationships within the legal framework of society offer only "indifferent justice", indifferent, that is, in being impartial, but indifferent also in being uncaring. Against this framework of society Muir sets the memory of his brothers playing. If ever there had been guilt in that memory, there is none now, only regret at his own dullness, regret that they took their separate ways all those years ago:

> A darkness covered every head
> Frowns twisted the original face,
> And through that mask we could not see
> The beauty and the buried grace.

The poet knows now that it was a paradise they left. He dreams that his dead brothers are in another paradise, a paradise like the first but also different, for Muir gives implicit acceptance to the traditional idea that paradise is both the place of our first innocence and the place to which we aspire. Though Edwin, the living brother, can recall their first paradise, he is not ready for the new one:

> A brightness poured from head to head,
> So strong I could not see their eyes
> Or look into their paradise.

This brightness is the brightness of the flaming sword that guards the east of the garden of Eden to prevent the return of Adam and Eve. The poet knows that he cannot return from exile. Yet the vision of that first paradise will always be with him. It is a vision that reflects the shared experience of boyhood with his brothers. If Muir approaches the metaphysical here he does so only obliquely, and he stops short of a broad statement of faith. The final statement of the poem, in which he reverts to the ballad traditon, combines fact, mystery and faith. It is as carefully limited in its scope as it is confident in its tone:

> And in a vision I have seen
> My brothers playing on the green.

According to his autobiography, the poet's earliest memory was that of being baptised in Wyre at the age of three. He remembered being dressed in a scarlet suit with gold buttons, and he remembered also that the minister who baptised him was Mr Pirie, who had come over from Rousay for the occasion.[28] Just why the ceremony was postponed until he was three years old is not clear. Such delay was not normal. John Firth testifies that baptism usually took place in Orkney at that time as soon as possible after birth.[29] The United Presbyterian Church, to which the Muir family belonged, ruled that it was "the duty of the session to see that all the children of church members are baptised without unnecessary delay."[30] But this did not happen in the case of Muir, and even the record of the baptism takes a rather casual form, stating only the name of the child, the names of the father and the minister, and the year (1889). No dates of birth or baptism are given, nor the name of the mother, though all of these are normally to be found in baptismal records of the time.[31] One can only assume that Mr Pirie brought his records up to date some time after the event and never got round to collecting all the information. The Muirs were, of course, comparative newcomers to the district and Mrs Muir's maiden name would not generally be known.

As it happens, there exists another account of the baptism. In 1966 Ernest Marwick interviewed a lady of 92, Mrs Craigie, who had been present at the poet's baptism and remembered it well.[32] She recalled that Edwin wore a sailor suit for the occasion, which hardly supports his memory of its being scarlet. It did, however, have "lovely bright buttons". And Muir did remember having a sailor suit. Some sixty years later (according to *An Autobiography*) or forty (according to *The Story and the Fable*)[33] the memory of a sailor suit came into Muir's mind and, with it, the certainty that he had once worn it; yet he could not remember when he had worn it and he still had a separate memory of the scarlet suit he had worn at his baptism.[34] Muir is inconsistent about the date of the memory and it is probable that Mrs Craigie's memories of the baptism are more to be relied on than his own. The confusion indicates that the details of Muir's memories, for all their apparent immediacy and realism, may not always be literally accurate at all.

Muir appears to recall vividly the little world, close to the ground, in which he lived as a small child. He identifies the consequences of the child's view of the world from a height of only two or three feet:

> Grass, stones and insects are twice as near to him as they will be after he has grown up, and when I try to re-create my early childhood it seems to me that I was focussed on such things as these, and that I lived my life in a small, separate underworld, while the grown-ups walked on their long legs several feet above my head on a stage where every relation was different.[35]

That underworld contained its share of horror. The insects fascinated and terrified him.

One has to remember that the floors of Orkney farmhouses had, at that time, no carpets or even floorboards. Floors commonly consisted of beaten earth or of flagstones laid on the earth; insects were always present. John Firth, in his memories of the period, says:

> Very few houses could boast of any floor or pavement. The cold clay, devoid of any covering, carpet or rug, was deemed comfortable enough for man as well as beast.[36]

George Mackay Brown's experiences, some thirty years later than Muir's, were similar. "The first thing I remember," he wrote, "is the blue flagstones on the floor."[37] And Ernest Marwick recalled that a sheepskin rug was "the only comfortable place in that cold area of stone" and that the box bed was the only refuge from the cockroaches that emerged from the flagstones.[38]

The little world at the floor of the Bu, closer to nature than that in which most people grow up, remained a very real memory to Muir. The insects came into his dreams.[39] They came also into his poetry. One example is in "The Refugees":

> A crack ran through our hearthstone long ago,
> And from that fissure we watched gently grow
> The tame domesticated danger.

Another, perhaps, is in "The Combat", which describes a battle between two monsters, monsters that can as well belong to the insect world as any other:

It was not meant for human eye,
That combat on the shabby patch
Of clods and trampled turf that lies
Somewhere between the sodden skies
For eye of toad or adder to catch.

The memory of the floor of the Bu, or that of Garth where "worms writhed up between the flags in wet weather",[40] provides also the material for a striking image in *Poor Tom*. Mansie, walking in Glasgow, sees the crowds on the pavements on either side of the street as being on two rafts, borne past one another on a river, each heading for an unimaginable destination:

> These two rafts bearing all that human freightage floated just a little above the world, were only a thin partition over a bottomless quagmire, and through the planks the mud oozed up and clung to the passengers' shoe-soles, though their heads were so high in the air.[41]

The image has the quality of nightmare, but it derives from experience—the experience both of the young man in Glasgow and that of the child in Orkney watching the worms ooze up between the flagstones. The experience has been subjected to the processes of the poetic imagination, perhaps assisted by dreams and by the workings of the unconscious; but it is impossible not to conclude that the raw material is drawn in the first place from concrete experience. There is no need to view Muir as the passive recipient of messages from the unconscious. The experience of his childhood, imperfectly remembered though the details often were, was intense enough to inform his poetry for the rest of his life.

Chapter Four

# THE FARM

MUIR'S FATHER did not go out to work. He did not have an office, an overseer, or a trade union. His work was not something held in a special compartment of his life, to be compensated for by an element of free time: it was, rather, a framework, or one of the frameworks, of his existence and that of his family. For young Edwin Muir the farm was not simply the place where his father worked: it was the basis of their family life.

Only when he was grown up did Muir learn that distinction between work and leisure which, since the Industrial Revolution, most men have taken for granted. One response he made to the distinction is an uncharacteristically ironic poem, "Suburban Dream". In this poem, a visitor to the suburbs one summer afternoon observes the children and the women at their leisurely pursuits and knows that

> The men are all away in offices,
> Committee-rooms, laboratories, banks,
>     Or pushing cotton goods
>     In Wick or Ilfracombe.

With "the masters gone" there is a kind of peace, but one that will come to an end with the afternoon:

> But soon the brazen evening clocks will bring
> The tramp of feet and brisk
> Fanfare of motor horns
> And the masters come.

Elizabeth Huberman praises the "anti-masculine insight" of this poem which she reads as a statement of support for exploited women.[1] But one can, I think, read the poem in this way only at the expense of much of its irony. The bathos of "pushing cotton

44

goods" ensures that the reader is not over-impressed by the importance of the work of "the masters"; and the ostentatious manner of their return home at the end of the day suggests a lack of sympathy on the author's part. But the world which all this activity pays for—"the cool elysium" of "women, schoolgirls, children, garden talks"—gets its own share of ironic treatment. It is not a world for adults, but only "a child's dream of a grown-up world". The choice of the word "elysium" for the afternoon world of the suburbs, where the children play Chopin and read history books while their fathers perform apparently meaningless tasks in strange places, suggests an ambivalent attitude towards it. It is both a paradise and a place where the inhabitants are not truly living. Muir is not taking sides between the men and their families but is, rather, questioning the arrangement that divides them. The suggestion is that the families have as little understanding of offices and banks as the men have of Chopin and history books.

The division between work and leisure, between the lives of men and their families, is foreign, not only to the life the Muirs enjoyed in Wyre, but to traditional peasant communities the world over. S.H. Franklin, in his study of the remaining peasant communities in Europe, concludes that the objectives of the typical peasant farm, in which all members of the family are employed (and he might have been speaking of the Bu in Wyre), are "primary genealogical and only secondarily economic" and that "those things which belong to the kinship order—family, status, marriage and death, are inextricably mixed with those things that belong to the economic order: occupation, inheritance and property."[2] Collier's work on the crofting "problem" in Scotland reaches similar conclusions.

To recognize the non-economic aspects of peasant farming is not, of course, to urge the sentimental view of the peasant as one content with his lot and somehow immune from the avarice that besets the rest of us. The objectives of peasant agriculture listed by Franklin are entirely compatible with the desire for material possessions. One has only to read the statements made by crofters to the Napier Commission and to the Crofters Commission to see that the crofters could be as grasping and cunning as their landlords. But their evidence equally makes it clear that they envisaged their economic opportunities within their total way of life and not just within the context of employment.

Outsiders might calculate that the association of the kinship and economic orders is, in the long term, inimical to economic progress; but it does offer a kind of freedom which the peasants themselves seem to value. Sometimes that freedom is viewed unrealistically, as by the respondent in a survey quoted by Franklin: "I'm a free man, and we don't have to get up in the morning like the factory workers."[3]

The Muirs certainly had to get up in the morning and the poet is under no illusions about it:

> I watch the farmstead on the little hill,
> That seems to mutter: 'Here is my day again'
> Unwillingly. Now the sad cattle wake
> In every byre and stall,
> The ploughboy stirs in the loft, the farmer groans
> And feels the day like a familiar ache
> Deep in his body, though the house is dark.
>
> *The Wayside Station*

These lines have the authentic voice of experience. Muir had none of the townsman's illusions about the pleasures of farm work. Work remains work, remains the "familiar ache", even where there are no masters. Moreover, the land and the climate can be formidable enemies. Yet there is a satisfaction to be had from carrying on the work of generations, and of doing so within the living family.

The genealogical objectives of the peasant family are outlined, without sentimentality, in "The Difficult Land". The poem begins with the blunt admission that nature can be a hard taskmaster, indifferent to the will of man:

> This is a difficult land. Here things miscarry
> Whether we care, or do not care enough.
> The grain may pine, the harlot weed grow haughty,
> Sun, rain, and frost alike conspire against us:
> You'd think there was malice in the very air.

It is not surprising that men give way to frustration:

> We shake our fists and kick the ground in anger.

One of the things that keeps them going is that feeling for the
ancestral heritage which is part of the genealogical approach to
work:

> We are a people; race and speech support us,
> Ancestral rite and custom, roof and tree,
> Our songs that tell of our triumphs and disasters
> (Fleeting alike), continuance of fold and hearth,
> Our names and callings, wake and rest and sleep,
> And something that, defeated, still endures—
> These things sustain us.

Another is the support of the family, all members of which are
enrolled in the enterprise, for better or worse and for the whole of
their lives; so that when, at times, they are tempted to abandon
the land, and with it their very identity, they are

> drawn back again
> By faces of goodness, faithful masks of sorrow,
> Honesty, kindness, courage, fidelity,
> The love that lasts a life's time.

The land itself and the passing of the seasons have a hold over
them too; and, mysteriously, the living have a responsibility to the
dead

> Who lodge in us so strangely, unremembered,
> Yet in their place.

Thus the poem lists the motives of the peasant as Muir reads
them: his feeling for ancestral custom, his love for his family, his
identification with the natural world, and his sense of responsibility towards the "unremembered" dead. These feelings unite
into a conviction of the rightness and inevitability of the way of
life:

> This is a difficult country, and our home.

In adopting the paradox that a man can be motivated by
necessity and that a way of life is right because it is inevitable,

Muir is in harmony with the less articulated assumptions of those who faced pressure to abandon that way of life. As will be seen in Chapter Ten, the common assumption of the crofters who emigrated to Canada during the nineteenth century was that once they were there, they would re-create the way of life they had known in the Highlands of Scotland. Their aspirations, inevitably, were controlled by their experience. The conviction stated in "The Difficult Land" is that one cannot abandon one's experience without at the same time abandoning one's identity. From that Muir moves to the more questionable view that what is inevitable must be right, so making a virtue of lack of choice.

The contrast with the world portrayed in "Suburban Dream" is marked. In the suburbs there is a wealth of choice. The men can choose from a variety of occupations in offices, committee-rooms, laboratories and banks; their wives and children can fill their afternoons with a number of leisure activities. Yet the poem implies that these activities do not add up to a satisfactory whole or even offer the kind of freedom that one might expect from having choice. During the day there is choice of a kind: the absence of the men-folk "liberates" the keys of the piano and "sets free" Chopin, but every action behind the "idle doors" seems to exist on some kind of purposeless periphery and can be halted by the return of the men. The return of "the masters" creates a distinct feeling of unease. The "tramp of feet" suggests more an invading army than a re-union of loved ones. The "fanfare of motor horns" announces the arrival of great, and therefore alien, beings, not the meeting of equals.

The struggles of the farmers in "The Difficult Land" are, in contrast, sustained by love, love both of the kind that "lasts a life's time" and that which goes out to the whole race:

> For how can we reject
> The long last look on the ever-dying face
> Turned backward from the other side of time?
> And how offend the dead and shame the living
> By these despairs? And how refrain from love?

The dislocated life of the industrial world offers none of these supports against despair. Instead, Muir seems to be telling us, home and work are mutually alien, families are better apart, and

the customs of the past reach us only through the medium of Art.
Of course, this suburban world of Chopin and history books lacks
the apparent sordidness of the Glasgow to which the Muirs
emigrated. But the difference is, in a sense, superficial, because
the fact of exile

> (leaving behind
> Name, body, country, speech, vocation, faith)

involves loss of identity and so is a kind of death. The houses of
the "Suburban Dream" are not the kind of home Muir would
recognize. Home has to be on the soil of his ancestors.

The farmers, Muir tells us, "had customs which sanctioned
their instinctive feelings for the earth."[4] These feelings were
surely passed on to the poet. He was given to using images of
cultivation, suggesting, for example, that every poet is given "a
patch of ground which he is at liberty to cultivate",[5] and devoting
a whole poem, "The Place of Light and Darkness" to an image of
a resurrection that is a harvest gathered by "the great husband-
man". He writes in his diary of his love of "ploughed fields,
especially of harvest fields, and stacks where all is gathered—the
most satisfying sight there is."[6] Within this imagery it is virtually
impossible to disentangle the experience of the boy in Wyre from
later literary influences on him.

His satisfaction does not lie entirely in what is economically
productive. On a journey through Dumfriesshire he began to feel
that the land was too productive. He felt that the ground itself had
certain rights, felt by those who lived in close contact with the soil
and for whom ploughing and reaping were more than a business.[7]
How fanciful is this feeling? Mercea Eliade argues strongly that
there was once a universal belief that human beings are born of
the earth itself and that this primitive idea lingers on in an
obscure way even among Europeans today.[8] One is tempted to see
this idea in some of the statements made by crofters to the Napier
Commission in 1883. One certainly sees it in some of Muir's
poems.

At the very simplest level the poetry celebrates

> With homely smell of wine and corn and cattle,
> Byre, barn and stall, sweat-sactified smell of place.

*Moses*

And it confirms that

> Men are made of what is made,
> The meat, the drink, the life, the corn,
> Laid up by them, in them reborn.

*The Island*

This takes us beyond the merely secular and beyond the normal feelings of patriotism for one's country or district. The idea that food and life are laid up by men and are reborn in them, that men are made of what is made, approaches the primitive feeling of oneness with the soil identified by Eliade. It is a way of thinking not confined to Orkney and it is one that is being rediscovered and consciously revived by "environmentalists" in the second half of the twentieth century. But Edwin Muir must be the last British poet who could have absorbed such patterns of thought unconsciously as a boy while growing up in a society that was still attached to them.

Feelings for the natural world that go beyond the secular could survive in an agricultural community only because, as Muir says, ploughing and reaping were more than a business. The traditional feeling for the land was sanctified by customs that had no obvious economic motive.

Historians of religion tell us that the first farmers of the Neolithic Age adopted quite a different view of the world from that of the hunters who preceded them, turning to magic and religion to influence the growth of the crops.[9] So it would seem that from their first beginnings the activities of the farmers partook of the sacred along with the profane. There was little distinction between the tasks of technology and the magical or religious observances that went with them. All were justified by custom, by the actions of the ancestors. They fitted into the rhythm of the seasons; they would go on being repeated for ever. "The true 'fall into Time' begins," says Eliade, "with the secularization of work."[10] Muir, with some anguish, lived through just this process of secularization. His parents had lived a way of life that his own generation could only remember and evaluate. He could recognize the difference between those who lived in the old order and those country-lovers whom he met when he went for walks in the countryside around Glasgow. "What really drew them into the country," Muir decided, "was a personal or racial memory of a *protective order* which had existed before the modern chaos came upon us."[11]

What Muir thought of as a "protective order" still did exist to a considerable extent in the Wyre of his boyhood. There was joy still in the seasonal round, satisfaction in the celebration of the ritual. Recalled with affection in the autobiography are the long winter evenings when the cattle were gathered into the byre and the humans could devote themselves to story-telling, the wild day each spring when the cattle were released from the darkness of the byre to the new light of the fields, the sowing of the grain, and the rich colours of summer. Old customs fitted easily into these seasons, and thus survived.

Ernest Marwick was able to uncover, for example, a remarkable survival of magical technology in the use of the plough. The single-stilted Orkney plough, popularly supposed by the Orcadians to be that of the ancient Romans, was still in use in Muir's boyhood, though the iron plough was rapidly replacing it. It was a common practice to have a round stone hanging on a piece of string at the side of the plough; it had to hang at the side facing the sun and it was moved to make it do that every time the plough turned at the end of the furrow. By the end of the nineteenth century people would explain that the stone was necessary to keep the mouldboard of the plough clean, but Marwick, having examined several of these ploughs, insists that it could not have done that. It was, he suggests, a symbol of the sun: the stone was supposed to draw power from the sun and give it to the land.[12] Those who used the plough in the second half of the nineteenth century could hardly have believed in the magical effect of the stone, so they were forced to give its use a technological explanation that was more in keeping with the spirit of the times but which had no stronger foundation in fact than the old explanation. What, in effect, they were continuing to do was to perform a ritual act based on symbolism. So we have an example of symbolism used in a non-literary context within the lifetime of the poet.

Customs associated with the harvest were still widespread. An account of the harvest customs practised in Orkney at the end of the last century reads like a source book for *The Golden Bough*.

There was, for example, always great competition among the farmers in any particular district to avoid being the one to bring in the last sheaf. This last sheaf was the object of great superstition. It was often made into a straw dog or *Bikko* and left on the farmer's step to shame him; in some areas it was kept in the roof of the barn and fed to the mare and foal on New Year's morning.[13] A curious feature of these customs was that there was no surviving myth to justify them, so that they continued in a kind of limbo, faithfully practised until quite recent years but without any known reason.

The land and the harvest are two of the three great elements to which the farmers related. The third is the animal world.

To the town child animals are either familiar pets or exotic intruders. To Muir, the child, they were both closer and more mysterious. He admitted to "a passion for animals" and ascribed this passion to his having been brought up close to them.[14] But the passion came not merely from familiarity. Muir saw always the mystery of animals and their place at the heart of so much that is important in the life of man. The bringing of cows to the bull was "a ritual act of the tradition in which we have lived for thousands of years"; the annual killing of the pig was "a ceremony as objective as the rising and setting of the sun."[15]

Of all animals it is the horse that most interests Muir. His two poems, "Horses" and "The Horses", widely separated in the date of their composition, have attracted considerable critical attention. Both Butter and Huberman perceive, behind the intrusive archaisms and verbal awkwardness of the first of these poems, a strong feeling struggling for expression.[16] To describe this feeling Huberman uses the word "worship"; and this is a word that might aptly be applied in the later poem, if by "worship" is meant strong feelings of mystery, awe and reverence.

"Worship" is, in fact, Muir's own word for the emotion he felt as a child when his father and Sutherland brought the horses in from the field. He felt both terror and longing, a combination of emotions which added up to "worship in the Old Testament sense". The feeling was reinforced by a picture in a copy of *Gulliver's Travels* of a horse sitting on a throne judging a crowd of men.[17] Such was the impression that this picture made on Muir that he mentions it, not only in his autobiography but also in *Poor*

*Tom*, in which the hero, having seen the same picture, thinks of a horse as "the kingly judge".[18]

For Muir the horse is both the sign and agent of the conversion of the mundane into the miraculous. The horse seems to come from another world; it inspires both fear and love; it judges man. Such attributes are given to the horse in both poems, "Horses" and "The Horses".

In the earlier poem the horses "seemed terrible, so wild and strange"; they held "magic power"; their bodies were "seraphim of gold"; they glowed with "mysterious fire". They are clearly a symbol of the divine in that childhood Eden that is now faded.

The horses in the later poem are three times described as "strange". The survivors of the war that "put the world to sleep" are afraid of the horses and "did not dare go near them". As in the earlier poem, the horses are a divine presence. But the view-point of the poet has changed. He is now, not only looking back with nostalgia at an Eden that has faded, but, as in "The Brothers", he is looking forward to one that is to come. It is the classic double vision of Paradise: that which has been enjoyed in a legendary past but is lost for ever, and that which is yet to come. The vision of the past makes possible the vision of the future. It begins to seem to the survivors in the poem that the horses have been sent, that they have come from the lost Eden to help men recover Eden through going back to the ways of their ancestors, to the work of the land and the companionship of animals. One is bound to ask why horses should come to be presented, not merely as symbols of the good life, as reminders of the pastoral tradition, but as agents of transfiguration and salvation, as manifestations of the divine. The answer to this question may lie in ancient Scandinavian tradition and its survival in nineteenth century Orkney.

According to Marringer, the horse was the favourite sacrificial animal of the Germans in prehistoric times and symbolized the sky god. Davidson instances finds in Scandinavia to show the importance there of horse sacrifice in the fifth century. Turville-Petrie describes semi-Christian ceremonies involving horse sacrifice in Scandinavia during historic times.[19] Svale Solheim's comparative study of popular gatherings in Norway, Iceland and the Hebrides, in which horse races, horse fights and horse processions played a prominent part, shows how traditions described in the Sagas survived in certain remote areas of Scandinavia in the eighteenth and nineteenth centuries; and Solheim concludes that such ceremonies must have belonged to an ancient cult associated with the harvest.[20]

Solheim's book makes no reference to any horse traditions in Orkney but there is evidence of such traditions and certainly the importance attached to horses in Orkney is quite striking. The Norse name for the mainland of Orkney was *Hrossey*, which means "island of horses". At the time of the first Statistical Account (1798) there were 9000 horses in Orkney, a number which, according to William Thomson in his introduction to the 1978 reissue of the Account, was higher per arable acre than that of any other area in Europe.[21] Some of the original contributors to the Account recognize the disparity between the economic need for horses and the actual number. The contributor of the Evie and Rendall account notes that the number of horses in the parish was double that necessary for the work; the Rev. William Clouston, writing about the parish of Sandwick and Stromness, after suggesting that the number of horses would appear great when compared to the number of acres cultivated and the quantity of grain raised, goes on to give a reason for this extravagance and to describe a ceremony that is strikingly similar to those described by Solheim:

> It is the pride of the farmers to keep as many, and as good horses as they can afford, and therefore they give them a considerable part of the oat-crop. It is usual at a marriage, when returning from church, to try who can ride foremost to the wedding house, and they are as keen on the race, and perhaps as much elated with the victory, as those of higher rank are at Newmarket.[22]

This custom seems related to the Hebridean *Oda* which took place at Michaelmas, and which, according to Solheim, must derive from a Scandinavian autumn festival of prehistoric times.[23] If the horse ceremonies were originally associated with the harvest, as Solheim believes, it is easy to see why they should come to be associated with weddings. An association of the horse with fertility might also help to explain the Orkney taboo against riding mares which was noted by George Low in 1773. So strong was the prejudice against mares that, despite the number of horses kept, there was hardly any breeding of horses in Orkney until the nineteenth century, most stallions being until then imported. Even after breeding did become an acceptable practice, most foals were destroyed at birth.[24]

A custom which survives to this day is the boys' ploughing match in the island of South Ronaldsay. In this ceremony, young boys, dressed in elaborate costume, are paraded as "horses" before taking part in a miniature ploughing match on the beach. The purpose is clearly ritual rather than competitive.

Picturesque as this ceremony is, the most widespread survival in Orkney of the veneration of the horse is the secret Society of the Horseman's Word. Muir refers to the "Word" as an item of secret information which his father was supposed to have.[25] But the Horseman's Word was much more than that: in Muir's boyhood it was an active organization in which young farm workers secretly initiated one another into the mysteries of their craft in a ceremony that was half foolish, half solemn.[26] The ceremony was usually held about Martinmas (11 November) which would fit into the farming year at about the same point as the ceremonies described by Solheim. The Society was at one time known throughout Britain, but in the nineteenth century it was particularly widespread in North-East Scotland and Orkney. It appears to have been active in Sanday, where its membership included several neighbours of the Muirs of Colligarth.[27] That Edwin Muir does not mention there being a branch of the Society in Wyre suggests that the island was probably too small to sustain one, but it would seem that his father must have joined the Society in Sanday as a young man.

The origins, nature and purpose of the Horseman's Word are matters of conjecture and dispute. Evans believes that the Society had its origin in ancient fertility cults and that the attitude to horses implicit in the ceremonies is one of totemism or kinship. Macpherson regards it as the last surviving example of witchcraft and suggests that its central dogma was that there must be complete harmony between man and his horse. Carter, whose interest is more socio-economic than cultural, stresses the fact that nineteenth century observers saw the roots of the Society rather in the craft guilds than in witchcraft, and suggests that "cultural lumber" surviving from the days when witchcraft was being practised was drawn into the ceremonies in order to restrict access: it was, in effect, an early trade union designed to give farm workers the opportunity for communal action against their employers.[28]

Carter's thesis would not explain why it was so common in Orkney for farmers themselves and their sons to join it. The restriction on access seems to have been against the devout rather than against employers. A farmer told me in 1981 that none of his family had belonged to the Society because "they were all church folk". Others that I have spoken to have admitted their own membership in rather a shame-faced way. No-one to whom I have spoken in Orkney has shown any inclination to equate the Society with the National Union of Farmworkers.

What this adds up to is the central place of the horse in Orkney culture and an attitude to horses which is at once reverential (the horse represents another world) and familiar (the horse is man's companion in his daily work): the very attitude, that is, that informs "The Horses", in which men achieve a new paradise through the recovery of "that long-lost archaic companionship" with the strange horses. "The Horses", forging—as does "The Brothers"—a link between this world and the Other, could have been written only by a poet steeped in the Orkney lore of the horse.

Chapter Five

# THE FABLE

In 1955 Edwin Muir travelled to the United States to deliver at Harvard the Charles Eliot Norton Lectures, which were later to be published under the title *The Estate of Poetry*. The audience at the first of these lectures must have been taken somewhat by surprise when the distinguished poet devoted part of his lecture to a detailed explanation of the role of poetry among the people of the island of Wyre, and when he did so moreover in terms which could leave them in no doubt that, in the visiting professor's view, the Orkney peasants of 1890 had had a better understanding of the nature of poetry than had the academic students of English literature in 1955:

> I was brought up in a group of islands on the north of Scotland, remote enough for life to have remained almost unchanged for 200 years. In our farmhouse in one of the smaller Orkney islands, there were not many books apart from the Bible, *The Pilgrim's Progress*, and the poems of Burns. Except for Burns we had no poetry books, but we knew a great number of ballads and songs which had been handed down from generation to generation. These, sometimes with the airs traditionally belonging to them, were known in all the farms; there must have been hundreds of them. They were part of our life, all the more because we knew them by heart, and had not acquired but inherited them.

He went on, a little sardonically, to equate "literature" with the local newspaper, which arrived weekly by boat, and concluded that the community in which he had been brought up was a more civilized one than could easily be found in the middle of the twentieth century because the peasants had preserved for hundreds of years a treasury of poetry, including song, which was regarded, not as something special, but as a normal part of life.

57

There may be some element of tactical exaggeration in all this, designed to give strength to a critical point about the nature of poetry; and one has to allow also for Muir's instinct to see

> My youth to myself grown fabulous
> As an old land's memories.

*Day and Night*

But certain things are given as facts and have to be taken as such: the family had few books, but hundreds of traditional songs were known to them and their neighbours; these songs were part of an oral tradition and were known by heart; they were at one and the same time both highly prized and yet not considered anything out of the ordinary.

These statements are in harmony with the comment in *An Autobiography* that the neighbours of the Muir family "had a culture made up of legend, folk-song, and the poetry and prose of the Bible."[1] The picture that emerges—of a civilized community enjoying a living oral culture that was more integrated with people's lives than anything that comes out of a public library—is an attractive one. But is it true? Just how strong was the oral tradition in the Orkney of the last two decades of the nineteenth century? And how does it relate, if at all, to Muir's output?

The traditional songs, of which Muir says his family knew hundreds, have now all but disappeared. Balfour published a collection of songs drawn from the island of Shapinsay in 1888. Balfour was exceptional in collecting songs in Orkney, though it was being done with dedication elsewhere. The great mass of Orkney songs has disappeared without trace. A correspondence in the *Orcadian* in the winter of 1933-1934 attracted the submission of many songs, but most of them proved to be either Scottish or modern.

Ballads have survived rather better, partly because the ballad collectors active at the end of the last century did manage to cast their nets as far as Orkney, partly because the ballads seem to have survived in the memories of old people rather longer than the songs. The most celebrated collection of ballads is that of F.J. Child (published 1882-1898), but a collection more relevant to the Orkney scene is that of Gavin Greig, which was published in

1925. Greig had two Orkney contributors (both from Sanday): T.S.Towers, who submitted versions of "The Bailie's Daughter of Islington" and "Sir James the Rose"; and J.A.Fotheringham, who contributed a version of "The Dowie Dens o' Yarrow".

Of these, "Sir James the Rose" (or "Ross") seems to have been a particular favourite in Orkney. Alan Bruford, recording in Orkney on behalf of the School of Scottish Studies of Edinburgh University in 1970-1971, found several people who could sing it to him. Muir quotes its opening lines in his autobiography and says that after learning it from his mother when he was a child he had never come across it again; yet there is an eye-witness account of his having sung it in a farmhouse in Stenness during his last visit to Orkney in 1956, a performance which suggests a remarkable memory for verse. Many years earlier, at the age of four, he had sung at a concert in Wyre another of his mother's ballads, of which he was able to quote in the autobiography the last four lines, it was "Hind Horn".[2]

The other ballads that enjoyed a particular popularity in Orkney were "Binorie" and "Sir Patrick Spens", and there were persistent traditions that both have an Orkney origin. A version of "Binorie" recorded by Bruford in Orkney in 1966 is typical of the Aberdeenshire versions collected by Greig but does have significant variations of its own. In 1970 Bruford collected a peculiarly Orkney version of "Sir Patrick Spens" from a man in Burray who had learned it from his father but who was unable to avoid confusing parts of it with a literary version he had learned at school. Child mentions, with some scepticism, the local tradition that the grave of Sir Patrick Spens is situated in Papa Westray in Orkney.[3]

Although ballads have never been collected in Orkney in the systematic way that they have been in the North East of Scotland, there is ample evidence that they were in wide circulation until the end of the nineteenth century. So were songs. Muir tells us that his mother was fond of singing both "sacred" and "carnal" songs. He was acutely aware of the difference between traditional and printed songs and of the greater confidence with which the former were sung. He was himself a good singer.[4]

At least as important as the retention of ballads and songs was the habit of telling stories round the fire on winter evenings. The custom is firmly entrenched in local mythology and has inspired the title of a collection of tales gathered by C.M. Costie, *Around the Orkney Peat Fires*. The sentimental nostalgia with which this custom has been surrounded in an age when people sit round the television set should not be allowed to diminish its significance. That it survived until almost the end of the nineteenth century may have had something to do with the comparative lack of books. Dennison, whose educated contemporaries took their culture from outside the islands, writes of the Orkney peasants' fondness for "any mental enjoyment suited to their uncultivated capacities" and adds that, in the absence of books, "this taste was gratified, and abundantly cultivated, by hearing and reciting their own traditions, by the fireside, in the long winter nights of their northern clime."[5]

It is a commonplace that there can be no culture without leisure and it seems likely that the long winter nights and the enforced rest from farmwork that resulted from them were important factors in the maintenance of the oral tradition. John Firth bears witness to an enforced leisure that is hardly known today:

> After the crop had been secured in the corn-yard, and the thatch on all the houses had been renewed so as to withstand the winter storms, there was, during winter, little work for the farmer of sixty years ago compared with what he of the present has to do.[6]

Firth goes on to say that during these long winter evenings the women had indoor work to do but the men "could smoke and doze and 'spin Yarns' by the fireside."[7]

In a sense, the "yarns" may have been no more than time-killers, but the effect of such oral literature on those who participated should not be underestimated. Dennison remembers seeing an old woman who lived in poverty and squalor, describing a mermaid to a group of children:

> The old woman seemed wholly absorbed by the beauty of the being she described; her hands dropped on her knees, her eyes glowed with the enthusiasm imparted from her description; and from the manner in which she emphasised her laudatory words, you could not but for the moment believe that she had seen with her own eyes the charming creature she

described, while we youngsters, with eyes wide open and
gaping mouths, sat around her, spell-bound, believing every
word she said.[8]

Muir had first-hand experience of communal story-telling. He
remembered the stories around the fireside at the Bu, and
particularly his father's stories of the supernatural. There is no
doubt that he was, in J.C.Hall's words, "still able to draw upon a
pastoral tradition which is now almost extinct in the western
world."[9]

Many of these stories told around the fireside were stories of
local life; but there were other tales, clearly of more ancient
origin, which indicate belief in fairies, trows (the Orkney version
of the Scandinavian trolls) and Fin-folk (an undersea people).
George Robertson of Yesnaby collected tales about these creatures in 1884, a collection which has never been published.[10]
Robertson disclaims any belief in these stories on his own part,
but says that he knows people who do believe in them. Such belief
always appears slightly in the past (a favourite phrase of
Robertson's is "in the writer's memory") and one is reminded of
Katharine Briggs' comment that fairy beliefs have always been
supposed to belong to the last generation and lost to one's own.[11]

In Robertson's memory, for example, there were old people
who believed that the ocean was inhabited by a race of people
whom they called "Fin-folk" and these old people would caution
the young whenever they went near the shore to keep their faces
turned always towards the sea in case the Fin-folk took them
unawares and carried them off to their land beneath the sea.
Robertson knew a woman who was convinced that her late
husband was alive and well among the fairies. A hundred years
later a man from South Walls told Ernest Marwick that his great-
grandfather knew a man who had spent a year among the trows.[12]
So belief in a parallel world is sustained.

Ernest Marwick had contact with several people who put belief
in a parallel world much less far in the past. A lady in Shapinsay
gave him in 1958 a vivid recollection of seeing a fairy when she
was small; he was told of a member of staff of the laundry in
Kirkwall who never ate her "piece" until she had broken off part
of it and put it outside the window for the fairies; and he was
assured that an old man who had sold a piece of land some time in

the 1960s had been most anxious that the buyer should not plough the "howie" (burial mound) for fear of disturbing the fairies.

What these stories seem to have in common is the belief that there are other, fugitive, races sharing our world, and these are confused with historical peoples. Thus burial mounds, which are common in Orkney are said to be the homes of trows or fairies; fairies are sometimes associated with the Picts; and the Fin-folk are confused with the Lapps or Finns who were often thought by the Norse people to have supernatural powers.

The most important collector of Orkney folk-lore was undoubtedly Walter Traill Dennison (1826-1894) of Sanday. Dennison's attitude to what most other educated Orkneymen of his day regarded as outworn and useless superstition was one of patience and sympathy. He realized that the peasants were well aware of the contempt in which their stories were held and that they would repeat them only to those who would not sneer at them. Listening patiently to the often tedious repetition of old tales Dennison was struck by the fact that both the story-tellers and their audience believed in them.[13]

Dennison's sympathetic yet unsentimental account reads as reliable evidence both of the importance of story-telling and of the sincerity of the narrators. Of the mysterious land of Finfolkaheem, he writes: "Though situated at the bottom of the sea, I have heard it more minutely described than any well known city is in the pages of a gazetteer."[14]

So we have fabulous anthropology, fabulous genealogy, and fabulous geography. And for a people constrained socially and geographically, the world is thus ordered in a satisfying pattern. A world of fabulous races, fabulous lands, and fabulous creatures offers more varied material to the imagination than that suggested by the small croft. The closeness of the other world to this one meant that the Orkney of Muir's youth was, in his own words, "a place where there was no great distinction between the ordinary and the fabulous" and he gives by way of example that a man he knew once set out in a boat to meet a mermaid and claimed afterwards that he had talked with her.[15] Muir does not give the man's name, but he was probably William Delday, a neighbour of the Muirs at the time they lived at Garth. The Deerness mermaid was seen by several people in the autumn of 1892 and Delday actually announced his intention of marrying her, after which unkind people said she was never seen again.[16]

Was there also a literary tradition among the Orcadians to match the folk-lore tradition? Marwick's *An Anthology of Orkney Verse* prints poems by some 36 Orkney poets, ranging from Rognvald Kolson of the twelfth century to Edwin Muir of the twentieth. It is an impressive anthology to be drawn from a community that today numbers only 18,000 people and which probably never at any time exceeded double that figure.

The greatest poets of Orkney's past were undoubtedly those of the Norse period. Rognvald Kolson (1104?-1159), the Earl who led a pilgrimage to Jerusalem and who built Saint Magnus Cathedral in Kirkwall, was a gifted poet. Bjarni Kolbeinson (who died in 1222), who lived in the Bu long before the Muir family moved there, produced the most celebrated of all Orkney poems, "The lay of the Jomsvikings". Some scholars have claimed that certain of the poems contained in the great collection of Icelandic verse, the *Elder Edda*, were written in Orkney.[17]

It is, however, a prose work, *The Orkneyinga Saga*, that is the best remembered work of literature from Norse times in Orkney. This work is an Icelandic Saga with Orkney subject-matter; and, though there is no certain evidence of its having been written in Orkney, Professor Stombeck of Uppsala, at a conference held in 1968, argued that certain passages in it could have been written only by authors having a detailed knowledge of, for example, the topography of Rousay.[18] At the time of the Saga's composition Orkney was part of a Norse world that was producing a corpus of literature destined to have a permanent and world-wide significance.

Cultural decline came with the annexation of the islands by Scotland, the change of the language from Norse to Scots, and the imposition of a new religion, when, to use George Mackay Brown's words, "the ballads and songs went down before the rants of John Knox."[19] Muir, who himself had no high opinion of Knox or what he represented, maintained that the ballads owed their inspiration to a view of life that is older than Protestantism.[20]

Towards the end of the nineteenth century Walter Traill Dennison commented sadly that nothing remained in Orkney of

Norse literature except the bare bones of some of the old heroic stories and garbled versions of some of the poems. Being less hostile to Knox than either Brown or Muir, he ascribed this decline to the loss of the language. It was through the change from Norse to Scots, he suggested, that the poetic element of the stories was lost.[21]

Dennison's argument seems entirely plausible. Yet there are those, including Muir himself, who have argued that certain characteristics of the old Norse language have carried over into the kind of English spoken in Orkney today. Muir claimed that the speech of his Orkney neighbours retained the inflexion of the language used in the Norwegian valleys from which their ancestors came—an inflexion that was musical, slightly melancholy, but companionable, "a splendid voice for telling stories."[22]

The Norse language disappeared neither so early nor so suddenly as might be supposed. George Barry, writing in 1805, reports a conversation in Norse between two old men in the parish of Harray, which took place in 1756 or 1757. Dennison records an accepted belief of his own day that the "Danska Tong" survived for two centuries after the annexation of the islands by Scotland and was still understood by old people in the middle of the eighteenth century. In support of the idea that there was some sort of carry-over from this language to the English spoken by the Orcadians of today, Geipel has identified in the speech of modern Orcadians certain patterns of intonation and some non-English locutions which have Scandinavian prototypes.[23]

The memory of the old literature has, however, with a few exceptions such as "the Play o' de Lathie Odivere", faded over the centuries. The last survival of Norse literature known generally by the people of the islands is thought to have been the poem which Gray paraphrased as "The Fatal Sisters" and which the minister of North Ronaldsay was astonished to discover was known by heart among his parishioners in its original language some time after the publication of Gray's poem. By the time that Muir was born it seems certain that little direct knowledge of the great literature of Orkney's past could have been widespread. But there was certainly a large body of oral literature that would be known to Muir, and there was a spoken language well equipped to be the vehicle of a new literature.

Yet, even if one allows the formative influences on Muir of the traditional awareness of language and the fondness for story-telling that characterized the community in which he lived, one may still ask whether he made very much use of the actual subject matter of the oral tradition.

Daniel Hoffman, who has studied Muir in relation to Yeats and Graves, is convinced that Muir makes little or no use of the wealth of folk material that was available to him, material of the kind that both Yeats and Graves had to discover for themselves by laborious study, and that he turns instead to Troy and Greece for the material of his personal myth.[24] A weakness of Hoffman's argument is that his knowledge of Orkney folklore seems to be restricted to the fairly superficial rehash of traditional tales that is to be found in Gorrie's popular travel book, *Summers and Winters in the Orkneys*. Better guides to the material available to Muir are Greig's *Last Leaves of Traditional Ballads and Ballad Airs* (1925), Marwick's *The Folklore of Orkney and Shetland* (1975) and, above all, Dennison's *Orcadian Sketchbook* (1880) and *Orkney Folk Lore and Tradition* (edited Marwick 1961).

Dennison, a farmer of some substance in the island of Sanday, was a writer of rather insipid Victorian verse before he started transcribing, often in dialect, the tales that he heard around him. Muir, an immeasurably greater poet, began, one might say, where Dennison left off. One should not look in his work for the transcription of traditional materials, but these materials are sometimes, especially in the early poems, clearly visible. One might take as examples two stories that are re-told by Dennison (though they do not appear in so well known a collection of Norse tales as that by Desant) and which are remembered in Orkney even today. They are "The Stoor Worm" and "The Mester Ship"

The Stoor Worm, a sea creature of mysterious origin, was the most terrible of living animals. Its tongue alone was hundreds of miles long. It fed on seven young maidens every week. To rid themselves of this burden the people sought the advice of a spayman or soothsayer who told them that the creature would go away if the king's daughter were sacrificed to it. The king, of course, had no choice but to agree to this inconvenient arrang-ment, but he managed to obtain a period of respite during which he advertised far and wide that he would give his daughter and his kingdom to anyone who would kill the worm. On the very last day a hero came forward, Mester Assipattle by name, who entered the creature's mouth in a boat and destroyed it by setting fire to its liver.

So far this story has a familiar ring. Almost every part of the world has its monster that devoured maidens before being destroyed by a hero. What is particularly interesting about the Orkney story, however, is the manner of the creature's death. So terrible were its dying agonies that its struggles almost capsized the world. Its tongue, having caught the moon, fell to the earth and created the sea between Denmark and Sweden. Its teeth formed the island group of Orkney, Shetland and Faroe. Its body curled up and formed Iceland, where the smoke from its still-burning liver can sometimes be seen among the mountains.

One can identify this tale in Muir's early poem in the Scots dialect, "Ballad of the Flood", in which the flood is created, not by God, but by a "twining worm" that "wrapped itsel the warld around" and "brak the hills in pieces sma'". One finds it, too, used in a more symbolic way, in a much later poem, "The Song". Professor Wiseman, who regards this poem as one of Muir's finest, devotes several pages of his book to a thoughtful study of it. Granted that it is indeed a highly symbolist poem, Wiseman's statement that it remains "unlocated within myth, biography or any known symbology" goes too far in removing the poem from recognizable signposts. The mysterious creature of the poem surely owes something to Muir's memory of the Stoor Worm.

As is often the case with Muir, the poem draws upon and inter-relates an old memory and a recent dream:

> I was haunted all that day by memories knocking
> At a disused, deaf, dead door of my mind
> Sealed up for forty years by myself and time.

These lines suggest that the poem derives from what the unconscious has made of real memories. The material is given form by the device of a reported dream. The phrase that Muir uses to open the second stanza of "The Song" ("That night I dreamed") echoes the conventional opening line of "Ballad of the Flood". The dream of "The Song" is of

> the resonant moaning
> Of some great beast in anguish.

When the moaning ceases the poet wonders what was the message
that this vision has for the world:

> What wound in the world's side and we unknowing
> Lay open and bleeding now? What present anguish
> Drew that long dirge from the earth-haunting marvel?

It is hardly possible that this creature, forever dying, does not owe
at least something to the Stoor Worm, hardly likely that the belief
that the creature has visited the earth with a warning of disaster is
not related to the connection that Muir had earlier made of the
Stoor Worm with the Flood.

In short, the mysterious creature of "The Song" belongs, not to
some private or arbitrary symbology, but to a traditional story;
and it is interesting that Muir connects what is essentially a
creation myth with warnings of ultimate disaster.

A second example of a folk-tale that seems to have had an
influence on Muir's work is "The Mester Ship". Like the worm,
this ship was vast—so vast that when the stem was lying off
Stronsay (the neighbouring island to Sanday) she was at the same
time taking on a cargo of wood amidships off the coast of Norway.
There is not really any story attached to the Mester Ship; there is,
rather, a series of anecdotes calculated to demonstrate its immense
size. For instance, the captain told a young lad standing beside
him in the stern to go forward to the bows and tell the men there
to weigh anchor. In Dennison's version

> When he left the captain he was a well-favoured young man,
> with bright, yellow hair, and cheeks as red as a harvest moon,
> and when he came back aft he was a bowed down old man,
> with white hair, and cheeks as grey as a tanned hide.[25]

Another story tells that a knife dropped by a seaman working on
one of the yards had rusted to pieces before it reached the deck.

At first sight such tales may appear no more than tall stories,
expressing a delight in exaggeration and paradox. But the way
that distance is inferred by the passage of time and illustrated by

concrete images shows an imaginative awareness of the relationship between space and time; there is, too, in the ageing of the seaman and the rusting of the knife, a real feeling for the mutability of earthly things.

In "The Voyage" Muir uses a ship to draw on this same theme of time and space. The sailors in the poem have journeyed for so long that they fear there may be no-one else alive on earth when they make landfall. The situation is a development of that found in the story of the Mester Ship. Moreover, what the traditional tale gives the poet is not merely the stark outline of the story, but also the beginnings of a dramatic response to it.

The same sort of fear of what might have happened during a long absence is found in "The Return" and in "The Strange Return".

"Time is a sea", writes Muir in Part VII of *Variations on a Time Theme*, and continues,

> There, if I could but sail
> For ever and outface Death's bullying gale
> I'd ask no more.

Yet in "The Voyage" the sailors are terrified that they may indeed be sailing for ever while the rest of the world reaches its consummation. It is just this awe of endless time, this fascination with, and fear of, eternity, that informs the various anecdotes associated with the Mester Ship. It is a theme, too, constantly at work in Muir's poetry.

So it would be wrong to suppose that Muir uses no traditional Orkney material in his work. He was certainly aware of such material and he seems to have absorbed it into his work in such a way that it is transmuted into symbol. What he took from Orkney folklore was less a collection of tales than a habitual grasp of the relationship between the visible and the invisible.

Willa Muir identifies the ultimate contribution of Orkney folklore to Muir's poetry as follows:

> As a child in Orkney, which was then not very far from the
> Middle Ages, Muir had lived in an atmosphere saturated with
> legend, myth, ballads, and Bible stories. There was some kind
> of accepted story to account for everything. It was natural for

him to look for a great story, an all-encompassing myth, to explain the mystery of life as he later found it.[26]

Willa Muir probably romanticizes the real situation in Orkney at the time of her husband's childhood. She herself was brought up elsewhere. But what she writes must be evidence of what her husband thought about the prevalence of traditional myths in Orkney during his boyhood. Her remarks are, in particular, an interesting indication of the origins of Muir's search for "a great story". The search is a prominent element in his work. It begins in Orkney.

To the impact of all this folklore one must add the impact of Muir's reading. The autobiography indicates three stages in his boyhood reading. When he was very small and living in Wyre the books which were to be found in the house and which stirred his imagination were *The Pilgrim's Progress*, *The Scots Worthies* (a collection of exciting, if badly-written, stories of the Covenanters), and, of course, the Bible. He remembered also very vividly a weekly magazine to which his family subscribed, the *Christian Herald*.[27] This periodical was not, as one might have supposed, a main-stream Protestant family magazine. It consisted largely of what its advertisements called "prophetic articles", most of them written by the editor, the Rev. M. Baxter. Baxter was convinced that the end of the world would occur on 11 April 1901 and that it would be preceded by such wonders as the dismemberment of the Ottoman Empire, a world war, and the rise to power of the last great anti-Christ, who would be none other than Prince Jerome Bonapart. These events would be followed by one thousand years of peace—the Millenium. This was heady stuff, and we know that these speculations sank deep into the young Muir's mind.[28] The Millenium was to be a recurring theme in his poetry.

The second phase of his reading that Muir was able to identify later occurred when he was nine. At that age he read everything he could lay his eyes on, but what was available was "poor stuff without a vestige of nourishment, and it did not leave a trace behind."[29]

Then at the age of twelve he discovered poetry—*The Excursion*, *The Eve of Saint Agnes*, and Arnold's *Tristan and Iseult*; and he realized it could be made out of things he himself knew. He made up his mind to be an author.[30]

The selection of works available to the budding author was obviously restricted. Yet it was enough to let him catch sight of the mystery of books. The reverent attitude to the language itself which Muir sensed among his neighbours perhaps joined with a feeling towards the printed word of reverence bordering on fear. James Muir had many stories about the Book of the Black Arts, a book which gave great power to its possessor, but which brought damnation to anyone who owned it at the time of his death. It could not be destroyed, and could be sold only at a lower price than its owner paid for it. In Muir's version of the story the Book could be sold only for a silver coin, and Edwin could not remember what happened to the poor servant girl who had paid a threepenny piece for it.[31] In the 1950s and 1960s many people were able to tell Ernest Marwick about the Book: one person recalled a story that the Rev. Charles Clouston (who died in 1884), to whom the Book had been taken in desperation by its last possible purchaser, buried it successfully in his garden by putting a Bible on top of it.[32]

One of the most important fruits of Muir's reading was a knowledge of the mythology of ancient Greece. In his *Collected Poems* there are about twenty poems in which the main subject-matter is drawn from classical material, and there are several other poems that refer, directly or obliquely, to Greek themes. This is a smaller proportion of Muir's output than an overall impression of his work suggests. It may be that Muir comes across as a poet who has absorbed the Greek tradition simply because some of his "Greek" poems are among his best:

> She wove and unwove and wove and did not know
> That even then Odysseus on the long
> And winding road of the world was on his way.
>
> *The Return of Odysseus*

> Forgiveness, truth, atonement, all
> Our love at once—till we could dare
> At last to turn our heads and see
> The poor ghost of Eurydice
> Still sitting in her silver chair,

Alone in Hades' empty hall.

*Orpheus' Dream*

In fact Muir uses only a small number of Greek themes, of which by far the most prominent are the desolation that is to come (or has come) to Troy, and the return of Odysseus from his travels. He has two poems on Oedipus and two on Prometheus, as well as the beautiful lyric on the story of Orpheus, quoted above, but by and large the Greek contributor to Muir's work is Homer.

Muir made no pretence of having a classical education. What fired his imagination, at the age of twelve, was Morris's *The Earthly Paradise*; significantly he saw his discovery of the classical world in terms of finding "a new race", rather than in events or themes, and significantly too he confesses that "even the Greek stories unfolded for me in a landscape very like Orkney."[33] It may be that Muir seems able to use figures like Penelope and Odysseus without giving the reader the feeling of an awkward literary intrusion because he puts them in a landscape which is so natural to his imagination and because he uses only those Greek themes that are so basic as to have parallels in Muir's native mythology. Even the story of Orpheus exists in a Shetland version, complete with Norse refrain, with which it is possible that Muir was familiar.[34] Willa Muir has pointed to the parallel between Homer's story of the return of Odysseus and the ballad of "Hind Horn" with which we do know Muir was familiar. The hero of the ballad has been sent abroad to stop him seeing the king's daughter; when he learns that she is to marry another he comes back, changes clothes with a beggar, and turns up at the wedding to claim his bride. It was part of this ballad that Muir sang at a concert when he was four years old. Doesn't the story sound familiar? asks Willa Muir.[35]

Muir succeeded in giving a universal significance to the situations that he took from folk-tales and from his early reading. His theory (to which he clearly attached considerable importance) that behind the recitation of everyday experience (the "story") lies a more universal statement of reality (the "fable") is the justification of much of his poetry. It is quite clear from his autobiography that Muir did not think he could live without myth and equally clear from his poetry that he could hardly write without it. He would have agreed with Jung that myth is what links man with his past. Muir remembered—or believed he remembered—a unified culture in the Orkney of his boyhood. He believed that it had once been universal and he gathered any remnants of it that came his way into poems that reflect that universality. His use of traditonal material is less self-conscious than that of Yeats because he had himself grown up in a community that still understood its relationship with nature and with the past. The myths, dreams and symbols which pervade his work are what most strongly relate it to life in Orkney.

It would be easy to exaggerate the completeness of the folklore heritage and the significance of its place in the life of the community in the Orkney of the 1890s. The tradition of story-telling around the fireside, knowledge of the substance of many old tales, beliefs that amounted to the recognition of another, only partly-visible world—all of these still existed, but Willa Muir's comment that the Orkney of her husband's boyhood was "not very far from the Middle Ages" goes too far. What Muir caught of the reality of the world of the imagination in the lives of the people around him was almost a dying glance. Walter Traill Dennison had already concluded that "the channels through which folk-tales have come down to us are now fast drying up"; for this he blamed cheap literature and advanced education.[36] That Muir knew the story of the Stoor Worm only from the pages of an almanac is revealing.[37]

At the time many rejoiced at the disappearance of folklore and did their best to hasten its departure. A certain Mr Whyte, for instance, toured Orkney in 1856 lecturing on "The Mental and Moral Improvement of the Working Classes". In Birsay, according to the *Orcadian*, he "lectured on popular Superstitions, showing the absurdity of a belief in witchcraft, fairies, ghosts, hobgoblins, and the whole of the superstitious ideas derived from the idolatrous religion of our ancestors". That he felt it necessary to lecture in such a way does suggest that superstition was in quite a healthy state in 1856; the newspaper itself regretted that "so few of the class for whose benefit the lectures were delivered were in attendance" and expressed its fear that "the old wives of the neighourhood are as superstitious as they were before."[38]

Where Mr Whyte failed, the 1872 Education Act succeeded. The teachers who were appointed as a result of the Act, and the ministers who often controlled them, having done their worst, Mr Goodfellow, minister in South Ronaldsay, was able to report in 1912:

> Times have changed, surroundings are different, and the atmosphere seems to be healthier, and life itself more wholesome. People are more practical and less sentimental, they have less time to muse on the past, or to be amused with fairy tales. The Hill Trows, the Water Trows, and even the Kirk Trows, have nearly all disappeared before the advance of light and truth. Perhaps we are all indebted to the Penny Post, the daily papers, and the weekly steamers, than anything else for the disappearance of the old fairies. The best way to dispel darkness is to pour in light.[39]

Science, too, played its part. Ernest Marwick, in his unpublished autobiography, *The Sufficient Place*, writes of the profound psychological effect on his neighbourhood of the opening by archaeologists of a green mound, the home, it was believed, of the fairies: the mound, he thought, had linked the people of the world of their ancestors, and now the sense of mystery had been dissipated.

One has to conclude, perhaps regretfully, that it is not true to say, as Willa Muir does, that "Edwin had lived in an atmosphere saturated with legend, myth, ballads, and bible stories." Edwin lived in an atmosphere in which Bible stories had certainly survived but in which the memories of legend and myth were being destroyed by the enmity of rationalist ministers. It was a time of transition, and the position of the Muir family in that transition was typical: James Muir had a great fund of tales of the supernatural and even claimed to have known several witches personally, and at the same time the family looked forward to the weekly visit of the steamer bringing the local paper, the very institution which Mr Goodfellow identified as the destroyer of superstition. It may have been a fortunate position for the poet: close enough to the traditional sources for him to absorb them, far enough from them to appreciate their value.

One can refer to two poems which show an appreciation of this special position: "Complaint of the Dying Peasantry" and "The Emblem".

"Complaint of the Dying Peasantry" is a somewhat didactic
poem, and it is difficult to disagree with Wiseman's view that its
presentation of a lost Eden in purely nostalgic and sociological
terms does little justice to Muir's thought.[40] The poem does,
however, have two interesting features. The first is that, although
the poet appears at the outset to be about to launch an onslaught
on the modern mass media ("Our sons are newspapermen"), the
real targets are quickly seen to be the scholars who wrote down
the oral traditions in literary form ("Sir Patrick Spens shut in a
book"). His criticism is directed at "Scott and Hogg, the robbers"
but it could as easily be pointed at Dennison and Greig, because
the charge against Scott and Hogg is not that they "improved" the
texts they collected, but that they collected them at all. Muir was
no doubt aware of the rebuke issued to Scott by Hogg's mother
that by writing down her ballads he had "broken the charm". The
second interesting feature of "Complaint of the Dying Peasantry"
is that the subject matter is not simply nostalgia for the lives of
those who had lived before the destruction of their culture, but
also distress for the survivors of it:

> But we are with Helen dead
> And with Sir Patrick lost at sea.

Muir's handling of this material is slightly clumsy, but the poem
does explain why Muir never made it his business to re-tell
traditonal stories. To capture them in print is to silence them.

"The Emblem" takes a more optimistic approach. Muir insists
here that the world of the fable is not, after all, dead. It has not
even contracted. If you enter its gate (which you pass daily) it will
grow so vast

> That this will seem a little tangled field.
> For you will be in very truth with all
> In their own place and honour, row on row.

The modern world has not, then, really diminished the accessi-
bility of the world of the imagination. To find it requires some
humility ("you incline your head"). The conclusion that Muir
reaches is close to that of Eliade, for whom myths are still to be
found everywhere, though degraded.[41]

This may take us to the point where some explanation may be
offered for Muir's comparative lack of overt reference to traditional material. Merely to preserve, in an alien form, the content
of oral material, is to destroy it. It will be destroyed whether the
poet faithfully records what he hears or adopts the common
twentieth century expedient of investing ancient myths with
peculiarly modern significance, for "modern" is not equivalent to
"universal". The real object of the poet is to preserve, not the
content of traditional material, but the insights which produced it
and which derive from a particular way of life. Muir owed his
ability to recognize that way of life for what it was, and to
appreciate its most significant elements, to the fact that it had
survived into the Orkney of his boyhood, was dying there even as
he left the islands, and was not to be found elsewhere.

That way of life, remembered from boyhood, identified in the
first of the Harvard lectures, touched on in the novels, and
described in the autobiography, informs the great mass of his
poetry.

Chapter Six

# THE ESTATE

EDUCATION and increased contact with the outside world changed the cultural outlook and activities of the people of Wyre: they had an even more profound effect on the islanders' economic activities.

Muir sometimes gives the impression that the way of life in Wyre never changed. The qualities of tranquillity, harmony and timelessness—qualities that appealed to him throughout his life—characterized life in Wyre as he saw it. The island, he claims, was "remote enough for life to have remained almost unchanged for two hundred years."[1] Leaving the place was some kind of time-accident, as though he had left Orkney in 1751 and arrived in Glasgow in 1901.[2] Most commentators on the relevance of Muir's life to his poetry have accepted his view of the unchanging life of Wyre as having historical justification. J.C. Hall, for example, suggests that *An Autobiography* gives us a picture of Orkney at a time when it was a "relatively primitive community."[3] Hall expresses some caution by using the word "relatively"; Christopher Wiseman goes further in suggesting that when Muir was a boy Orkney was "virtually untouched by progress and industry."[4] And Professor Butter, in the earlier of his two books on Muir, makes the same point even more strongly. "Around this ordered and united home," he writes, "was an ordered, non-competitive community, untouched by industrialism."[5]

This picture of a stable, happy community is an attractive one. But it should be viewed with caution. The very presence of the Muir family in Wyre implies that the community was not unchanging. James Muir was an outsider who came to the island in the hope of bettering himself. He failed. Notions of "progress" brought him to the island, and "progress" drove him away again. There was nothing timeless about the movements of the Muir family.

To a small boy the community in Wyre seemed self-contained. Yet the economic framework of all their lives was a wider one than the community of the island: it was the estate of Rousay and Wyre. The estate, comprising almost every house and almost every acre of land in the two islands, belonged to one man. According to the "Old" Statistical Account, there had been, in the 17th century, almost forty proprietors of these lands; but in the early years of the 19th century George William Traill, using money he had made in India, set about purchasing the lands of his neighbours; his heir, Frederick Traill Burroughs, carried on the same policy until in 1853 he became virtually the sole owner of the two islands. The "laird", as he was known, was a man of great power. Almost every family rented his land and lived in his houses. There was no restriction on the level of rent he could charge, no security of tenure for his tenants, and no alternative housing or employment.[6]

Most families had lived on their small crofts for generations. Until the middle of the 19th century formal leases were almost unknown. Tenancies were inherited; and they were paid for, not by cash, but by occasional service on the owner's farm. The peasants planted their crops in narrow strips of land (the "run-rig" system) and kept their animals on the common pasture on the side of the hill. This feudal, almost mediaeval, way of life is described in some detail in the "New" Statistical Account of 1842, and its disadvantages are listed again and again by the contributors to that Account. One of these writers, Robert Scarth, served as factor, first in North Ronaldsay and later on the Rousay and Wyre estate. He was a strong and intelligent advocate of "improvements". It was he, as well as the lairds that he served, who saw to it that timelessness was not allowed to remain a feature of life in the islands.

Reforms were undoubtedly overdue. Muir's observation that life in Wyre had not changed for two hundred years would have been substantially true in 1840, though it was certainly not true of the island as he knew it fifty years later. Pringle, writing in 1874 from his own recollections, says that agriculture in Orkney was not only backward in comparison with that in neighbouring counties but that "it was in nearly as primitive a state as it must have been when the islands were given as a mortgage for the marriage portion of the Princess Margaret of Denmark on her union with James III of Scotland."[7]

When change did come it came with vigour. The pioneer was Samuel Laing, a scholar as well as landowner, and translator of the *Heimskringla*. Laing carried out improvements on his estate in Sanday that were to be a model for others. He reclaimed, he drained, he enclosed the fields, he stopped the common grazing, and he assigned a few acres of land to each of his tenants. It was the beginning of the end of communal activity; every individual was now to cultivate his own bit of land. As a young man Scarth had worked with Laing, and Scarth carried out similar measures in the island of North Ronaldsay and in Wyre. Wyre thus became the most "improved" part of the Rousay estate. The improvements made it possible for James Muir to come in from outside. He did not have to inherit a traditional croft with its rights and obligations. He had only to offer the highest bid for the lease of one of the farms.

What gave Scarth and others the opportunity to make changes was the coming of the steamship. In 1833 the steamer *Velocity* began a fortnightly voyage between Orkney and Leith, replacing sailing vessels that had taken two or three weeks for the single voyage. She was the first of many such vessels. Farmers in Orkney could now abandon subsistence agriculture and become specialists. The climate of Orkney is peculiarly suited to growing grass and therefore to breeding cattle. It is notably unsuited to the growing of grain. The introduction of a steamer service to Leith meant that farmers could now export cattle and import the cheap grain that was becoming available from the colonies. For the first time there was an incentive to improve the breed of cattle through abandoning the common grazings.

Internal communication began to improve at the same time. When Robert Scarth became factor in North Ronaldsay there was, according to the "New" Statistical Account, "but one cart in the island, which was never used, as the horse showed some disinclination to go into it.". There were few carts because there were few roads. Pringle says that before 1857 there was scarcely such a thing as a road in Orkney: manure was carried to the fields and grain to the market in "creels" (straw panniers) on the backs of horses. This was changed by the Orkney Roads Act of 1857. But Rousay was ahead of the rest of the county in this respect.

George William Traill, having found no roads in Rousay when he acquired the property, built a road around the island and maintained it under a curious arrangement by which the tenants provided unpaid labour for the road while the landlord met all the costs of the poor rate.

Probably because of the presence of Robert Scarth as factor, the Rousay estate was in the forefront of other changes too. In order to establish "improved" farms, Scarth cleared two large areas of Rousay—Quandale and Westness—of most of their inhabitants and carried out fencing and drainage on an impressive scale. The profits to the landlord were equally impressive: the profit on the farm of Westness in 1865 amounted to £863. This farm of 2,800 acres had been created out of land occupied at the time of the 1841 census by no fewer than 215 people. The sufferings of those evicted, many of whom attempted to build new houses and cultivate new land on the rough moor outside the enclosure walls, became a pervasive legend in Orkney.

The evictions are remembered even today. It is inconceivable that they did not contribute to a powerful myth within the community only forty or so years after they occurred. The myth must have been familiar to Muir as a boy. It appears unmistakably in "Outside Eden":

A few lead in their harvest still
By the ruined wall and broken gate.
Far inland shines the radiant hill.
Inviolable the empty gate,
Impassable the gaping wall;
And the mountain over all.

The evicted tenants of Quandale and Westness were the hapless victims of agricultural progress at a particular moment in history. Muir draws them into a general myth, one that absorbs the myth of the expulsion from Eden and at the same time reflects the experience of his own family. And there is reference in "the radiant hill" to an important symbol for Muir, the Transfiguration. But the direct concrete symbol is that of the evicted farmer, and—because Scarth's improvement did not in the end bring prosperity to the island—the landscape, even today, is recognizably that of Rousay. Rousay today is perhaps the most backward

and the most melancholy place in Orkney. It is an island of
deserted houses and broken walls; the hill which was once said to
be swarming with horses, cattle, sheep, pigs and geese is now an
empty moor.[8] Of the remaining inhabitants only "a few lead in
their harvest still."

These changes took place before Edwin Muir was born. Similar
changes had taken place in Sanday during the time that his father
lived there. The whole family was to experience the insecurity
brought about by progress.

The owner of the estate, General Sir Frederick William Traill
Burroughs, appears in *An Autobiography* and in one of Muir's
poems, "The Little General". Burroughs was an exotic import to
the islands. Of partly French, partly Irish, and partly English
descent, but with fairly remote connections with the Traill family
of Orkney, he had served with the British army in India before
coming to Orkney to take personal charge of his inheritance. His
history is recounted in entertaining and vivid detail in William
Thomson's *The Little General and the Rousay Crofters*. As a child,
Muir saw the General on one of his visits to Wyre but it seems
that he knew little about him. "The story went," writes Muir,
"that Burroughs, on account of his small stature, was first through
the breach at the relief of Lucknow." Many of his contemporaries,
including some of his tenants, were sceptical of the truth of that
story, but Thomson demonstrates that the weight of the evidence
is that Burroughs was indeed first through the breach and that
there is some substance in Burroughs' own belief that he was
unfairly deprived of the Victoria Cross. What is undeniable is that
Burroughs suffered from a sense of injustice and became convinced that his tenants were as unfair in their dealings with him as
the military authorities had been.

Problems arose because Burroughs never had enough money to
modernize the estate as much as he wished and because his
tenants were unable to give it to him. Traditionally money had
not been a problem in this remote part of the world. Rents had
been paid in kind, either by labour or produce. As late as 1840
some thirty per cent of the income to the estate was paid in this
way. But in 1883 all the rents were paid in cash and arrears were
mounting.

And so the relationship between man and his neighbour began
to turn on money obligations. The celebration of the harvest

safely gathered—the "harvest home"—began to lose its spiritual and ritual nature and became a calculation of profit and indebtedness. Muir may not actually have remembered a better time, but he knew of one:

> O I shall miss
> With one small breath these centuries
> Of harvest-home uncounted.
>
> *The Solitary Place*

By the 1870s every harvest-home was being carefully counted. Reading the Rousay and Wyre estate accounts of this period one is struck by the meticulous tabulation of crop-values, rents and arrears, all entered on sheets headed "crop of" and the year. To count the fruits of the earth in this way is to devalue them and to imply that there is no other wealth than the material one. "The Solitary Place" continues:

> I have known
> The mead, the bread,
> And the mounds of grain
> As half my riches.

Muir was a farmer's son: he does not despise a good harvest. The "mounds of grain" of this poem is an image found in other poems:

> See on the harvest fields of time
> The mountains heaped like sheaves.
>
> *The Mountains*

> He sees the hills of grain,
> A day all yellow and red, flowers, fruit and corn.
>
> *The Place of Light and Darkness*

> Your arms will clasp the gathered grain
> For your good time, and wield the flail
> In merry fire and summer hail.
> There stand the golden hills of corn.
>
> *The Island*

The image suggests man in harmony with nature, getting due reward for his work. It has nothing to do with rents or arrears.

But rents and arrears were foremost in the laird's mind. For him, the estate was an investment. His removal from the house of Westness, the home, according to the *Orkneyinga Saga*, of one Sigurd at the end of the eleventh century, and the centre of influence on the estate for many centuries, to a new gentleman's seat built for him in the latest baronial style was a deliberate and symbolic gesture. The new house had to be paid for. Burroughs began to squeeze the tenants. By 1880 their arrears amounted to a sum equal to one third of the total rental.

Burroughs was not alone in this attitude to his tenants. He was perhaps typical of his generation of Highland lairds. But the national mood was against him. When the Irish Land Act of 1881 conceded to a rebellious peasantry the right to security of tenure on their crofts and judicially determined rents, crofters in the Highlands of Scotland decided "to turn rebels" themselves in the hope of getting the same benefits. Public disorder led to the appointment in 1883 of a Royal Commission to review the grievances of crofters.[9] The Commission, under the chairmanship of Lord Napier, sat in Kirkwall in the summer of 1881 and listened patiently, as it had done elsewhere, to a series of complaints against the landlords. When the turn came of the Rousay tenants there were two incidents which were regarded at the time as nothing short of sensational: the spokesman for the crofters proved to be the Free Church minister of Rousay, the Rev. Archibald M'Callum, and the laird flatly refused to comply with Lord Napier's request that he promise to take no reprisals against any of his tenants who might give evidence. Burroughs was the only landlord in the Highlands to refuse to comply with this request, and he proved as good as his word. As soon as the Commission had concluded its hearings he evicted from their crofts two of his tenants who had given evidence. The people in Rousay split into two camps on the issue, Burroughs received threats of assassination, and the island achieved national fame.[10]

For several years there was something like a war of attrition between Burroughs and his tenants. The landlord bitterly challenged the evidence given by his tenants to the new Crofters Commission which reduced rents throughout the estate in 1888, he explored the possibility of charging one of them with perjury, and he threatened two of them with an action for theft when they exercised their traditional right to collect stones for repairing walls.[11]

It was into a community divided by economic conflict that the Muir family moved in 1889.

Edwin Muir is sometimes thought of as coming from a background of exceptional poverty. Kathleen Raine, a friend of the poet, maintained, for example, that "Edwin Muir came from the poorest of the poor."[12] Muir himself, with his instinctive sympathy for the community of the poor, wrote:

> Our fathers all were poor,
> Poorer our father's fathers.
>
> *The Fathers*

But poverty is relative. The Bu, with its 93 acres, was one of the largest farms on the estate, and the £60 which James Muir paid annually in rent would have seemed a fortune to most of the crofters. Wyre itself, low-lying and fertile, was in marked contrast to the hilly moorland of the larger island of Rousay. The improvements carried out by Robert Scarth had already taken Wyre out of the world of crofting, the new farms being of such a size as to put them outside the scope of the Crofters Act.

The £60 which James Muir offered for the Bu in 1889 was excessive. But it was only by offering such sums and taking the risk that went with them that an ambitious man could advance. Those who paid their £3 annual rental and kept a cow and a sheep had belonged to the community for generations; their holdings seldom changed hands. It was places like the Bu that were let on short leases to those who saw them as a route to advancement. Since a fresh bid had to be made every year or so and no preference was given to the sitting tenant, a feeling of insecurity must have been constant and the actual turn-over was considerable: half the farms in Wyre changed hands at least once between 1880 and 1889. So, contrary to what one might have expected, Wyre had in 1889, not a stable long-established community, but as shifting a population as it had today.

For the extent of competition for tenancies the evidence is conflicting. William Mainland, who left Rousay in 1883, said at his presentation supper that rents were high because there were a dozen competitors for every vacant farm and people bidded more than the farm was worth.[13] Yet at the hearing in Kirkwall of the Deer Forests Commission in 1892, Burroughs' agent complained that the local crofters would not bid for the larger farms and that there was some difficulty in finding tenants for them. The Bu was instanced as a farm currently vacant and being advertised without success.[14] The truth is that the Bu was not vacant in any real sense. It was occupied by the Muir family, but the lease was due for renewal and the landlord was hoping for better offers.

Besides meeting the £60 rent, Muir had to find the capital to buy stock. The crofters with one cow and one sheep were having difficulty in meeting rents of £3 per annum. Muir would have needed considerably more stock to raise a rent of twenty times that amount. But with £60 per annum going out in rent there was little cash left to stock the farm properly. It was a vicious circle. James Muir could not make the Bu pay. When the lease expired in 1893 he moved to the nearby farm of Helziegitha (pronounced "Helye"), a farm which cost him exactly half what he paid for the Bu. It was a considerable come-down. The move was from the best farm in Wyre to one of the poorest.

Of the family's departure from the estate, Muir says laconically, "My father was driven out of the Bu, which was a good farm, and then out of Helye, which was a bad one, by the exactions of the landlord."[15] This is a simplification. In a letter to Kathleen Raine he suggests that he "would have been a bad farmer as my father was."[16] That his father was a bad farmer may not have been the case at all. The failure of James Muir's farming enterprise on the Rousay and Wyre estate may be ascribed to high rents, to a lack of working capital, to a series of bad harvests, and to his misfortune in moving to Wyre at the very time that the agricultural depression hit Orkney hardest. He might have weathered the storm more successfully as a small crofter.

The depression was a national phenomenon. Its course is described in P.J. Perry's *British Farming in the Great Depression 1870-1914*. Orkney was no more immune from the problems that Perry describes than any other part of the country, though this was not always appreciated at the time. Burroughs himself had forecast in 1882 that the price of cattle would hold well and that a huge profit could be made from poultry. But by 1887 the factor,

Mr Murison (who had succeeded Robert Scarth), was writing to all tenants recognizing the hardship brought on them by the fall in the price of cattle and announcing a remission of ten per cent on all rents. Burroughs could not resist adding (the draft of the letter purporting to come from the factor is in Burroughs' own hand) that the depression was being experienced all over the world and by all classes of society and that "in Orkney we have much to be thankful for." Arrears of rent, which stood at exactly £1 for the whole estate in 1874, had reached £1014 by 1887. Burroughs' own farm of Trumland was experiencing the same difficulties. It showed a profit of only £15 in 1889, the year that James Muir took the lease of the Bu. In coming to the estate at that time James Muir was joining a declining enterprise.

Neither was the weather much help; in this respect James Muir was almost unbelievably unlucky during his time in Wyre. He arrived there in the year in which Orkney had suffered what a local newpaper described as the worst drought in living memory.[17] The summer of 1891 was, in contrast, the wettest since records began in 1827. The following year was exceptionally cold, though the summer was sunny and the harvest good. In both 1893 and 1894 there were gales of over 80 miles an hour. Orkney is known for its wind, but gales of that force are relatively uncommon—there were only twelve such gales between 1869 and 1908. We know from *An Autobiography* that one of these gales made a big impression on Edwin; this must have been the storm of October 1893, for it was the year of the loss of the Rousay post boat with the drowning of six people, including a mother and her three children. The sea was still running high when James Muir and Sutherland set out with their neighbours to search for bodies.[18] The summer of 1893 had been one of drought. *The Scotsman* reported in July that the hay crop in Orkney had been the lightest anyone could remember, and that the pasture was scorched and the cattle suffering. In January of the following year the *Orkney Herald* wondered if, after one wet and one dry year, the year to come would strike a happy mean. It did. The hay crop of 1884 was above average. But the cattle did not reach the expected price.

In June 1895 Burroughs advertised Helziegitha for the second time in twelve months. James Muir had given up the struggle.

The coming of the Muir family to Wyre had itself been a step in the agricultural revolution. Adam Collier, in his work on *The Crofting Problem*, makes the point that the croft was first and foremost an ancestral home (much as Muir saw it) and that it is not to be judged by strict agricultural standards. But there was no ancestral home for the Muirs in Wyre. Those commentators who, like Elizabeth Huberman, think of Muir as having "a childhood in a static communal society"[19] have reached mistaken conclusions about the nature of Orkney society in the 1880s. The period immediately before, and during, James Muir's tenancy of the Bu and Helziegitha was one of disturbing economic change and social conflict within the estate.

Muir himself tended to encourage a simplified approach to the external reality of his boyhood. We have seen how he told an American audience in 1955 that life in Wyre had remained almost unchanged for two hundred years. He made exactly the same claim to Stephen Spender in 1936. It can not have been a casual view.[20] Yet taken in anything even approaching a literal sense it is simply misleading. Similarly misleading is the much-quoted passage in *An Autobiography* in which he tells his readers that life at the Bu was virtually self-supporting.[21] The old way of life that his father had known as a boy in Sanday had certainly been self-supporting. But the Bu had to raise enough cash to pay the rent. When he writes about a society unchanged for two hundred years Muir is really writing about the world of his father's boyhood. No doubt his parents passed on to him the memory of those days. And no doubt they protected him from the evil knowledge of money, a knowledge that they had learned in their own lifetime. This appears to be the theme of "The Gate".

The situation in this poem is similar to that of "Childhood": the poet and his sister are sitting outside the walls of Cubbie Roo's Castle near the Bu. But on this occasion the poet is not looking into the distance, to "the unseen straits" and the "new shores". He is looking fearfully within, to the fortress itself:

> We sat, two children, warm against the wall
> Outside the towering stronghold of our fathers
> That frowned its stern security down upon us.
> We could not enter there. That fortress of life,
> Our safe protection, was too gross and strong
> For our unpractised palates.

The "stern security" is not all that it seems. The children have to be protected from what lies at the very centre of their existence:

> Yet our guardians
> Cherished our innocence with gentle hands,
> (They, who have long since lost their innocence,)
> And in grave play put on a childish mask
> Over their tell-tale faces, as in shame
> For the rich food that plumped their lusty bodies
> And made them strange as gods.

Elizabeth Huberman identifies the forbidden knowledge with the knowledge of sex, [22] a view perhaps justified by the words "gross" and "lusty" (though anyone from a community in which food was hard-won and not always plentiful might use such words strictly about the business of eating), but, in any case, the poem has a more general reference. That the parents became "strange as gods" recalls the promise of the serpent to Eve ("Your eyes shall be opened, and ye shall be as gods, knowing good and evil.") The first consequence of the knowledge of good and evil was the awareness by Adam and Eve that they were naked. The second consequence of the knowledge was that they were expelled from the garden. The knowledge, the first shame, came to them *inside* Eden. The knowledge of financial failure came to Muir's parents there in Wyre—not in Kirkwall, or Glasgow, but in Eden itself. Muir's memory of life in Wyre suggests that his parents kept the knowledge of good and evil from him. Or at least it does so at first sight. But "The Gate" suggests that Muir recognized the protection and co-operated with it. Even after acquiring the knowledge of good and evil, the poet can appreciate the earlier state of innocence:

> There was a time: we were young princelings then
> In artless state, with brows as bright and clear
> As morning light on a new morning land.
> We gave and took with innocent hands, not knowing
> If we were rich or poor, or thinking at all
> Of yours or mine: we were newcomers still.

*The Young Princes*

They were young princelings, not because they were rich, but because they did not know whether they were rich or poor.

The picture of his childhood drawn by Muir in his autobiography and in his poems is, at least to some extent, compensation for the unconscious awareness of the harsh reality of life on the estate, a reality that could be evaded by setting back the calendar by no more than half a century. Somehow Muir preserved from his childhood a certain innocence, an innocence drawn from the past rather than the present. It was, as George Mackay Brown has said, a heroic story:

> What tends to be forgotten is his toughness, his ruthlessness even, faced with the near-impossible task of keeping the early sources pure in the materialistic rubbishy world of the twentieth century. Against all the odds he succeeded.[23]

The story is heroic because more than a feat of memory was required. Muir had to do more than go beyond the grim experience of his adolescence; he had to recreate the real heritage of his childhood from the barbarism that had grown around the Bu in the years before he was born. This reconstruction could be carried out only by someone with the vision to separate the essential from the accidental. One reason why Muir was so tenacious in reconstructing the fable from the elements that he found in Wyre was that the fable was invisible in the horrors of life in Glasgow. That is the obvious reason. But another reason must have been that the fable was disappearing even in Wyre itself under the impact of the social and economic changes that made up the history of the estate in his early years. His work demonstrates that it was the myth fostered in the little world of the Bu, a world protected to some extent from the harsh realities that surrounded it, that allowed him as an adult to see every new experience from the vantage point of innocence.

Chapter Seven

# THE TRIBE

THE "Wyre" chapter of Muir's autobiography contains a marked
feeling for the presence of the other inhabitants of the island: the
musical Ritch family who had earlier been their neighbours in
Deerness; Freddie Sinclair, the boy with whom Edwin had a
fight; the little girl on a neighbouring farm with whom he struck
up a friendship; Hughie o' Habreck who built a yawl for them;
Old Fred of the shop; the teacher. They can all, with the
exception of Old Fred of the shop, be identified in the 1891
census return. The little girl, with whom he enjoyed "a friendship
more intimate than a friendship between two boys would have
been", must have been Lizzie Ritch, daughter of James Muir's
great friend. Muir must have been mistaken in supposing that the
fight with Freddie Sinclair took place after the removal of the
Muir family to Helye, because the Sinclairs themselves lived at
Helye.

Orkney was at that time made up of almost self-contained
communities, separated one from the other by water and moorland. Professor Ramsay, who toured the islands in 1873 in order
to report on their educational needs, wrote:

> In Orkney the population is extremely scattered. There are
> only two towns, and very few villages—the population being
> almost entirely fishing and agricultural. The holdings are for
> the most part small; and though of late years a good deal has
> been done in the way of consolidation of farms, still the gen-
> eral appearance of the cultivated part of the county is like that
> in many parts of Ireland—dotted over with houses every-
> where, but without any concentration of the people into
> villages.[1]

Being an island, Wyre was a particularly tight world. Muir
commented that "in an island everything is near, for compressed

within it are all the things which are spread out over a nation or a continent and there is no way of getting away from them."[2] In 1891 the island had 67 inhabitants. They must have formed an almost tribal group. The 67 people listed on the census return have, without exception, common Orkney names. Only one person is shown as having been born outside Orkney (and he in Shetland), and about two thirds were born either in Wyre or in the neighbouring islands of Rousay and Egilsay. The Muirs themselves formed the most prominent exception to this pattern. Yet, paradoxically, stability of tenure on the farms is not a feature. Of the 16 families living in Wyre in 1891, 10 had not been living there at the time of the 1881 census. For reasons that will be clear from the previous chapter, there was frequent movement from farm to farm within the island group and within Orkney generally. The apparently foot-loose Muirs were not a special case.

Muir's memory of the society around him at that time was one of neighbourliness, co-operation and hospitality. Most general accounts of Orkney at the time support this impression. Admittedly, a Free Church minister who visited Orkney about the middle of the nineteenth century was not impressed favourably by the manners of the inhabitants. "The Orcadians," he wrote, "want the simplicity and hospitality of the Shetlanders, and do not by any means impress the stranger so favourably." But this view is exceptional. More typical of the reaction of visitors to the people they met in Orkney are those of R.O.Pringle, who wrote that "the people naturally possess a courteous, kindly, cheerful disposition", of R. Menzies Fergusson, who observed that "all classes are noted for their politeness and hospitality", or of John Kerr, the school inspector, who found the people of both Orkney and Shetland extremely hospitable and possessing a character in which "industry, self-reliance, and courage are combined with the gentleness more frequently found in women".[3]

Kerr might well have been writing about James Muir, whose gentleness is recorded in his son's autobiography, or, indeed, of the poet himself, in whom gentleness was a noted quality. George Mackay Brown, for example, meeting the poet for the first time at Newbattle Abbey where he was warden, found him "simple and friendly". Walter Traill Dennison maintained that Orcadians, as a result of centuries of misrule, "have shown that they possess one quality essentially requisite in the character of every true gentleman—the power of controlling their own passions."[4] That observation may go some way towards explaining the self-restraint in Muir's work.

Although he records his fight with Freddie Sinclair, as well as an episode in which a "coarse and overbearing neighbour found his boat being tampered with by two young lads",[5] Muir tends to idealize community relationships on the island. His memory of Wyre undoubtedly provides the model for the ideal society portrayed in "The Good Town", a society in which

> The ivy grew
> From post to post across the prison door.

What sins they did have in Wyre, the poet thought, were those of the flesh (which he finds excusable) and not those of the spirit. A much-quoted passage in the autobiography reads:

> The farmers did not know ambition and the petty torments of ambition; they did not realize what competition was, though they lived at the end of Queen Victoria's reign; they helped one another with their work when help was required, follow-ing the old usage.[6]

Yet Eric Linklater states a quite opposite view:

> There is perhaps an excessive individualism in Orkney. A man will rely on himself, stubbornly and with jealous regard for his self-reliance, though to combine with neighbours would give him many advantages.[7]

These views cannot be reconciled. It is fair to say that Muir's boyhood lay closer to the common people than did that of the more middle-class Linklater, and Muir does strike one in general as a more reliable guide to the "old usage". At the same time, the social and economic changes that were taking place during the time that Muir lived in Wyre created an environment in which Linklater's portrait can be recognized.

It is significant that Muir should equate the social customs of his youth with old usages. He is characteristically the recipient of

tradition rather than the recorder of change. For him, right
behaviour comes from imitating others, from repeating archetypal
actions. The explanation of the goodness in "The Good Town" is

> Perhaps no more than this,
> That once the good men swayed our lives, and those
> Who copied them took a while the hue of goodness,
> A passing loan.

In *Scottish Journey* he writes of the "tradition" among Orkney
farmers of helping one another. Willa Muir, too, insists that co-
operative ways of living were "inherited". They were inherited
only among the tribe. Outside the tribe other forms of behaviour
were admired. When the family moved to Glasgow, his elder
brothers quickly grasped "the principle of this new society, which
was competition, not co-operation, as it had been in Orkney.";
Willie tried to explain to Edwin the law of this society, which
consisted, he said, "in looking after yourself". Years after his
move to Glasgow, Muir defined, in *Scottish Journey*, the difference between the principles of its citizens and those of Orkney:
"in the islands it was considered contemptible to steal a march on
your neighbour and tasteless to push yourself forward; but I
found that here these things were thought not only permissible
but a mark of virtue".[8]

Among the Orkney peasants an awareness of mutual dependence arose from the practical need to share skills and effort
and from the realization of shared hardships. The sharing of skills
and effort stands at the opposite pole from self-sufficiency and
competition. Ernest Marwick recorded his memory of a time
"when every second man had something he could do superbly
well" and was the man one would go to if one needed that
particular skill.[9] One is reminded of the man who built a boat for
the Muirs. These people were not trained specialists: they were
neighbours who had some self-acquired skill and who had gained
the respect of the community by putting it to the service of others.

"I am debtor to all, to all I am bounden," writes Muir in "The
Debtor", and he adds that his indebtedness runs not only to those
neighbours alive in his own day but to the neighbours who lived
there before him:

> On the backs of the dead,
> See, I am born, on lost errands led,
> By spent harvests nourished.

Such indebtedness gives cause, not for shame (as it would do in the competitive world), but for consolation:

> Forgotten prayers
> To gods forgotten bring blessings upon me.

The poem recalls Panurge's praise of debtors in Book Three of Rabalais: "This borrowing, owing, lending world is so good that when this act of feeling is over, it immediately thinks of lending to those who are not yet born, by that loan perpetuating itself."[10] The connection is probably more than coincidental. That Muir was familiar with Rabelais' work we know from references to it in *The Three Brothers*.

An important aspect of mutual indebtedness was the lack of social distinction. The Rev. James Leslie writes in the "Old" Statistical Account of social relationships in Rousay, Egilsay and Wyre:

> There is no difference in manners and habits between the
> cottager and the master of the farm. The master often turns to
> the cottager, and the cottager sometimes becomes the master.
> Their houses and their furniture are exactly the same. They
> all, without distinction, sit at the oar in their boats; and at
> land they all jointly perform the same labour and work. Youth
> and old age constitute the only distinction of rank. The old
> often are so reduced that they betake themselves to going
> from house to house for sustenance; and then they are well
> received; and it is not accounted beggary when they do so.

These were the conditions in the islands at the end of the eighteenth century. Marwick's autobiography suggests that there was little difference at the beginning of the twentieth. Marwick was told by his father, who frequently did a day's ploughing for a neighbour too poor to own a horse, and who found tactful ways of distributing church alms to the poor, that he must always accept food in a croft-house in order to show that there was no distinction between rich and poor.

There was mutual courtesy, too, between the farmers and the beggars. There were no beggars in Wyre (leaving aside the old people mentioned by Leslie) because of its isolation; but as soon as the Muir family had settled in the farm of Garth on the mainland of Orkney beggars came about the house. They were always taken in and given food. The willingness to extend hospitality to beggars and tinkers, who were often welcomed for bringing the news, is mentioned in many reminiscences collected by Marwick.[11]

It could be argued that men actually lose their individuality—or, rather, fail to achieve it—through membership of a close-knit community in which the approval of neighbours is a major objective and in which patterns of behaviour are decided by one's ancestors. In several of his poems, Muir seems to welcome this kind of submersion of the individual personality. What he fears is the anonymity, not of the tribe, but of the modern city:

> We saw the homeless waiting in the street
> Year after year,
> The always homeless,
> Nationless and nameless.

*The Refugees*

> I have passed through war and peace,
> Watched populations driven along the roads
> To emptiness, movements like bird-migrations
> Of races and great families, bare at the last,
> Equal in destitution.

*Soliloquy*

> We did not see and Moses did not see,
> The great disaster, exile, disapora ...
> Nor did we see, beyond, the ghetto rising,
> Toledo, Cracow, Vienna, Budapesth,
> Nor, had we seen, would we have known our people
> In the wild disguises of fantastic time,
> Packed in dense cities, wandering countless roads,
> And not a road in the world to lead them home.

*Moses*

This is the peculiarly modern nightmare of a man who had lived in Glasgow in the first decade of the twentieth century and in Prague in the second and fourth decades. The people who have been swept into the streams of refugees can no longer be recognized even by their own kin-folk.

None of this feeling for one's kin and the place they call home has anything to do with racialism or nationalism. In Muir's work "race" usually means the whole of mankind and "tribe" the particular group of people whose past one inherits. Belonging to a tribe does not necessarily involve feelings of hostility to the members of another. What is clear in many of his poems is that he sees man, not just as a struggling individual, but as a member of a tribe through which knowledge of the mysteries can be gained. Our individual lives have significance, he suggests, only if we can read into them "the universal patterns of human existence."[13]

His constant awareness of a pattern created in the past sets Muir apart from most of the poets of his generation. His wife explains:

> It would be difficult for any sensitive child to grow up in Orkney without being aware, not from schooling or other instruction but simply knowing from within inside himself, that a long line of people had lived there before him. These imagined predecessors had surely enchanted Edwin and made him the kind of poet he was.[14]

She adds that, whenever he felt discouraged, he had only to visit Orkney "to be again assured that the extension of the past into the present was no illusion." The poet himself wrote to Kathleen Raine that he thought he inherited "ancestral imagination" from Orkney.[15] He thought it important that in Orkney there were so many signs of one civilization following another over the centuries,[16] the very theme, that is, of "The West".

He had the same feeling in certain other places outside Orkney. In Rome he was deeply moved by the church of San Clemente. This attractive building consists of an eleventh century basilica, underneath which is to be found a church dating from the fourth century, and below that a first century house and a temple of Mithras. What struck him about it was the continuity of centuries given visible form. Not surprisingly, he felt the lack of such visible continuity in America.[17]

Man needs the experience of the past, which is nothing less than the experience of those related to him in the tribe, the experience of those who have tilled the same ground. For this reason Muir saw no virtue in revolution, either of the religious kind of the Reformation or of the more recent Marxist variety. "Mankind," he insisted, "has never had a clean sheet since Adam wrote the first line on it." A clean sheet, he decided, was no more than an empty sheet, and the history of revolutions shows that "man is a poor deviser and a poor writer when he is deprived of examples."[18]

These themes are explored in several poems:

> Then how do I stand?
> How can I here remake what there made me
> And makes me and remakes me still?
> Set a new mark? Circumvent history?
> Nothing can come of history but history.
>
> *The Wheel*

> Nothing yet was ever done
>   Till it was done again,
> And no man was ever one
>   Except through dead men.
>
> *Twice-Done, Once-Done*

> Harvests of men to men give birth.
> These the ancestral faces bred.
> And show us through a golden glass
> Dances and temples of the dead.
>
> *The Island*

> Into thirty centuries born,
> At home in them all but the very last,
> We meet ourselves at every turn
> In the long country of the past.
>
> *Into Thirty Centuries Born*

These poems endorse an anti-historical view of human existence. For Muir the past is not merely what happened. It is the experience of our tribe and therefore our own experience. The experience will go on being repeated so that "we meet ourselves at every turn".

The tranquility that came from absorption in the tribe was being gradually eroded in the 1880s and 1890s. The economic changes outlined in the previous chapter brought in their wake social changes no less disturbing to the traditional fabric of the community. These changes contained two main elements: the increasing impact of the outside world on Wyre and the growing tendency towards class distinctions among its inhabitants.

The unaccustomed wealth brought to the lairds of Orkney by the kelp boom at the beginning of the nineteenth century had led to significant changes in their manner of living. A contemporary traveller noted that they had built for themselves town houses in Kirkwall, that they aspired to a better standard of education for their children, and that they were adopting more sophisticated dress and customs.[19] They even began to travel abroad. George William Traill, Burroughs' kinsman and his predecessor as laird of Rousay, was found dead in the lavatory of his London club. The event was a telling, if macabre, demonstration of the proximity of Orkney to the rest of the world. William Thomson has pointed out that Burroughs' very presence in Orkney was the result of improved communications with the outside world. The place had now, he suggests, "that degree of remoteness which lent a certain romantic charm, no longer the complete isolation which made contact with polite society impossible."[20]

Robert Scarth had campaigned vigorously for a steamer to carry mail across the Pentland Firth between Scotland and Orkney, pointing out to the Commissioners of Supply that the existing system of sending mail by a series of open boats led to delays of as much as 14 days at a time. Scarth was listened to: the first mail steamer went into service in 1876. Even Wyre had its own post office by 1865.[21] In 1879 the newly-founded Rousay, Evie and Rendall Steam Navigation Company brought into service a small steamship, the *Lizzie Burroughs* (named after the laird's wife), to replace the sailing packets that had until then served the little island group. An advertisement in the *Orkney Herald* in 1888 shows the *Lizzie Burroughs* sailing between Rousay, Egilsay, Wyre, Gairsay, Rendall and Kirkwall at a single fare for deck passengers of one shilling.[22] It was almost certainly this vessel that carried the Muir family and their possessions when they moved to Wyre in 1889.

Since agricultural improvements came from outside, it was natural to assume an attitude of reverence to other ideas from the same source. One understands what Muir means when he writes that Fred, who kept the shop, had "Edinburgh manners". The laird and his bride came from a world very different from that inhabited by the Muir family:

> At the marriage of Lieutenant-Colonel Burroughs and Miss Geddes, which took place in Edinburgh on the 4th instant, we are informed that the bride wore a very beautiful gold brace-let, presented to her by the tenants' wives on the Colonel's estates of Rousay and Viera. The wedding was a splendid affair, and was attended by Miss Burroughs, from Westness, by Sir Edward Colebrook; Sir John and Lady Lillie; Dr and Mrs Watt of Woodwick; Mr George William Traill and Mrs Traill, and other relatives of the Colonel, and, of course, by many relatives and friends of the bride.[23]

On their arrival in the island, the couple were formally welcomed by the tenants who, in their turn, were invited inside the house for refreshments.[24] But the deference on the one side and the civility on the other could not bridge the social gulf. We have seen in the previous chapter how the laird's economic interests could not be reconciled with those of his tenants. The parties started, in any case, from a position of mutual social incomprehension. The local people had ancestors who had tilled the soil of Orkney for centuries. Burroughs and his forebears had served the Empire in India. His life was narrated in some detail in the *Orkney Herald* at the time of his death in 1905.[25] He was unquestionably brave, intelligent, and of strong moral character. He was well-connected. But in the Orkney islands he was a man without roots.

James Muir could hardly have realized it, but what he was observing in his dealings with the laird was a sample of the dying agonies of the landlord class. For all the outward polite forms, nineteenth century incomers like Burroughs could never have enjoyed the same respect as the established lairds. Agricultural improvements and payments of rents in cash were turning the lairds into rent collectors even before the Crofters Act. The Act, by restricting their power to increase rents and evict tenants, removed most of the lairds' leadership role.

In the angry manuscript notes, all in Burroughs' unmistakable handwriting, that one finds among the Rousay estate papers, one detects a resentment that goes beyond the frustrations of a business man who has seen opportunities for making money trimmed by legislation. Burroughs clearly resented his loss of power. He complained to the Crofters Commission:

> All my actions as a landed proprietor during the thirty years I have had my Estate in Orkney have been subjected to a rigid and malicious scrutiny and every act that could in any manner be twisted to my disadvantage has in measured terms been brought to bear against me. And although I have disproved all of these, yet I have been held up to execration by the Public Press. Had I been a Malefactor, excepting in the matter of being at large I could hardly have met with worse treatment than I have here. My crime has been that after a long and responsible Military Career, on my retirement from the active list of the Army instead of becoming an absentee proprietor and spending my retirement in more genial climes, I have for the last 10 years resided on my Estate and have built a new house and made my home on an island off the extreme North Coast of Scotland, where my wife and I devoted ourselves to doing all in our power for the welfare of all around us, and finding some who publicly stated that they have always opposed me and would oppose me to death I have declined to permit these persons to become my tenants.[26]

Burroughs regarded the restriction of his powers over his tenants as theft of his property. "No government," he stated in a letter to the press, "has any just right to set aside the teaching of the Decalogue."[27] To a crofter who had been given security of tenure by the Commission he wrote, "Your family took advantage of an unjust law to deprive me of my property."[28]

He developed an almost obsessive fondness for litigation. His solicitors' accounts show that he took frequent actions against tenants for arrears of rent, for "filching" land, for miscropping, and even, as we have seen, for stealing stones. Invariably he lost in court. His instructions to his factor show a similar approach: for example, "present tenant cannot be permitted to be an offerer! Continue advertising."[29]

The landlords were not dethroned overnight. Hunter, who chronicles the decline in their power in the Highlands, sees the undermining of faith in them as a slow process.[30] Even after the drama of the Napier Commission, Burroughs had his supporters both in and out of Rousay. The anonymous writer who, in a letter to the press, described him as a "shining light" to the inhabitants,[31] presumably was a visitor, possibly a guest at Trumland; and "an old soldier of the 93rd Highlanders" who sprang to Burroughs' defence in the pages of the *Orkney Herald* with the statement that "he was famed for his justice and humanity"[32] was remembering him as an officer, not as a landlord; but there were those on the island who also took his side. The most notable of these was a woman whose husband's family had worked at Trumland House. She told Ernest Marwick that she had burned all Burroughs' papers that had come into her hands because "the laird had always been good to wir folk and we were determined nobody wad ever go pokin' in tae the way he dealt wi' the crofters or ran the estate."[33]

In 1892 the laird, for all his alleged unpopularity, was elected to be the councillor for the island, the other candidate having stood down on the grounds that it was his "humble opinion that all the Proprietors should be on the counsel as they pay half the rates."[34] Despite this notice of surrender by the other candidate, the election, for technical reasons, still had to take place. The *Orkney Herald* described the election of Burroughs by 8 votes to 3 as "a farce", which no doubt it was; but the unwillingness of anyone to stand against the laird makes it clear that he still had some power.[35]

It should not be imagined that, without the laird, the peasants formed a united community. There were signs of many tensions among their ranks. For a start, isles folk were, according to John Firth, looked down on by the people of the Orkney mainland.[36] There was also mutual hostility, remembered by Marwick, between the "hill-folk" who occupied the poorest land and the "valley-folk" who rented the better, more low-lying farms. The former, who were permanent residents, resented the latter's tendency to move from the tenancy of one farm to another and their lack of belief in the old customs.[37] It has to be said that, poor as they were, the Muir family fell into the latter group.

The Crofters Act protected the position of those with very small holdings. It did not help tenant farmers like James Muir. On farms the size of the Bu or Helye the landlord could ask whatever rent an offerer was willing to pay, and the tenant had no security of tenure. Not surprisingly, an Orkney Farmers Association was founded in 1894 to protect the interests of these tenants. The landlords in their turn, to protect their interests both against the crofters and the farmers, formed the Orkney Landowners Association and submitted a Memorial to Parliament asking that Orkney be excluded from any future crofting legislation.[38]

At the other end of the social scale, landless labourers also began to attend to their rights. In 1894 someone calling himself "St Ola Cowboy" (a clear reference to the parish in which Kirkwall is situated) commented in a letter to the *Scotsman* that "the present is an age of grievances" and that, while the crofters had had their grievances redressed by legislation, ploughmen were still working thirteen hours a day. Two years later there was a proposal for a Ploughman's Union in Orkney, though it does not seem to have come to anything.[39]

"I spent my first fourteen years in Orkney, where I was not aware of class," Muir wrote to Philip O'Conner.[40]

Yet those fourteen years were a time of considerable social tension in Orkney. The united community still existed as an idea. But as a fact it was passing into history. The tribe was breaking up.

Chapter Eight

# THE CHURCH

WHEN the Rev. Alexander M'Callum arrived in Rousay in 1880 to
become minister of the Free Church, he was accorded the honour
of one of those dinners which marked the coming and going of
prominent members of the community. The laird, of course,
made a speech. "In this little isle of the sea," he said, "shut up in
our own little world as it were, it is greatly to the advantage of all
that we should live together in Christian harmony."[1] His words
contained an unconscious and prophetic irony: those present at
the dinner would soon find some difficulty in living together in
Christian harmony. When M'Callum left the island in 1889 there
was no farewell dinner.

There were three ministers in the parish when Muir was a boy.
He remembered Mr Pirie, who was minister of the United
Presbyterian Church, as possessing a "sweet and gracious nature";[2] yet, for all the poet's nostalgic urge to make an Eden round
the place of his boyhood, there is throughout his work not the
slightest suggestion that the Church might have had something to
do with it. On the contrary, the goodness of the place seems to
derive from a spiritual reservoir deeper than the Church as he
knew it. A great amount of his poetry is indisputably "religious",
and it is clear that he eventually developed a religious faith that
was specifically Christian. This was the one element of his
thought that he did not interpret as growing out of ideas first
nurtured in his childhood: his religious faith is portrayed as an
adult discovery. What might be attributed to his Orkney background is a purely negative aspect, a dislike of churches. "My
God is not that of the churches," he wrote to Sydney Schiff in
1939, "and I can reconcile myself to no church."[3] In 1940 he
wrote to William Soutar: "The difficulty with me is that I have
faith, but that I cannot belong to any one religious community."[4]
Ten years later, after living in Rome, he was perhaps able to relax
his independence from churches.

102

His wife insisted, after his death, that her husband had wanted nothing to do with churches, and in private criticised Professor Butter's 1966 book for over-emphasising the religious motifs in her husband's poetry. Ernest Marwick, on the other hand, remembered Muir telling him that if he ever found a church in which he could be happy, it would most probably be the Church of Rome.[5] If this falls short of a declaration of faith, it does indicate a considerable change of attitude. In his later years Muir was certainly drawn towards religious structures; in doing so, he was, uncharacteristically, not drawing on the early sources. The Orkney background, it seems, was not a religious one.

Yet outward appearances might lead one to suppose that it was. The picture of his parents that emerges from the pages of the autobiography is one of people with a respect for religion but without ostentatious piety or especially active church involvement. They attended church irregularly (partly because of the difficulty of getting to Rousay in rough weather); they said family prayers on Sundays (and by implication not on weekdays); they discussed the Bible a great deal; they enjoyed hymns and regarded "profane" literature as sinful. Probably they differed little in their attitude and in the degree of their involvement from most of their neighbours, except, that is, in one striking and perhaps significant respect. An examination of the records of the United Presbyterian congregations of Holm (of which James Muir was a member before going to Wyre), of Rousay, and of Kirkwall (of which he was a member before leaving Orkney altogether) reveals that James Muir never became an elder of the Church. This is quite surprising. He was clearly a respected man, he was the tenant of the largest farm in Wyre, he was just the kind of man one would have expected to have become an elder. Was he, like his son, just a little aloof from the formal structures of religion? Muir's reference to his father's "spontaneous piety", which he contrasts with his mother's "deep respect for religion", is a hint that this might be the case.[7]

The Presbyterian practice of transferring members from one congregation to another by granting, and recording the issue of, disjunction certificates allows one to track the Muir family from one place to another. James Muir joined the United Presbyterian congregation of Holm in 1876, his address being given in the Session Records as the Folly, Deerness. Deerness had no congregation of the United Presbyterian Church. His sister, Margaret, transferred to the Holm congregation in 1877. There is no record, however, of his wife's having joined this congregation, nor of her having joined the Rousay congregation with her husband when the family moved to Wyre. James Muir's own name does not feature in the list of communicants of the Rousay United Presbyterian Church. The family appear to have kept themselves slightly aloof from full commitment to church membership.

After the move from Wyre to the farm of Garth, some four miles from Kirkwall, James and Margaret again obtained disjunction certificates and attached themselves to the United Presbyterian congregation in Kirkwall. They were not, as Edwin Muir acknowledged in an article in the *Paterson Church Magazine* in December 1952, very frequent attenders. In that article the poet, while recalling that his father was "a very religious man", diplomatically excused his family's absences from church on the grounds of "time and space", but it is difficult to take this explanation at its face value when one reflects that Edwin made a daily journey on foot to the school which stood alongside the church.

It does seem unlikely that Muir's life-long distaste for "churches" could have resulted from excessive church going in his youth. The family appear to have had rather less involvement in the formal structure of the church than was common in Orkney at the time.

The ecclesiastical geography of Orkney in the nineteenth century reflects fairly accurately the general pattern of Scottish rural areas at that time. With the exception of small numbers of Roman Catholics and Episcopalians (very small indeed in Orkney where there were few Irish immigrants to swell the one group or landed gentry to swell the other), the Scottish people were almost exclusively Presbyterian in their allegiance, though everywhere divided into three competing denominations. The Church of Scotland (the Established church), the United Presbyterian Church, and the Free Church used almost identical systems of government, adhered at least in theory to almost identical theological beliefs, and conducted services on very similar lines. Hossack, writing on 1900 about the variety of denominations to be found in Kirkwall, was quite confident that the mass of adherents of all of them "cannot tell the difference in doctrine or discipline which separates them from their neighbours."[8] The United Presbyterian Church, to which the Muir family belonged, was unusually strong in Orkney generally, it being usually the case that its strength lay in small towns rather than in the countryside. Except in Orkney, there were few country congregations of the United Presbyterian Church north of the Highland line. Andrew Thomson, the historian of the Secession Church (from which, by union with the Relief Church, the United Presbyterian Church was founded in 1847), draws particular attention to Orkney as a place where the Secession made a greater impact than anywhere else.[9]

The Secession was the result of the expulsion of Ebenezer Erskine and three other ministers from the Church of Scotland in 1733. The four had demanded stricter adherence to orthodox Christian doctrine and the right of church members to elect their own ministers. The church that was founded by the four ministers in 1737 grew rapidly. When, in 1847, it united with the Relief Church, a smaller body with similar origins and outlook, the new Church numbered 518 congregations.

It was half a century after the founding of the Secession Church that the influence of Erskine and his companions was first felt in Orkney. The people, it seemed, had for long shared the view of the Rev. John Yule of Kirkwall that "if we are right, we are all right; if we are wrong, we are all wrong."[10] The first undermining of this sociable uniformity came in the last decade of the eighteenth century when a few citizens of Kirkwall began to hold private prayer meetings. Dissent made rapid progress after the visit to Orkney in 1797 of the preacher, James Haldane, and two companions. Haldane kept a journal in which he expressed a low opinion of the state of religion in the islands at the time. "The islands of Orkney," he wrote, "according to our information, which is rendered strongly credible by what we actually witnessed, have been, for a period beyond the memory of any man living ... as much in need of the true Gospel of Jesus Christ, as far as respects the preaching of it, as many of the islands of the Pacific Ocean." He noted that, because some parishes were divided by the sea, and because the churches were frequently in want of repair, and the pastors in want of zeal, many people saw their ministers seldom in the course of the year; a person from Egilsay complained to him that the island had heard only three sermons in six years.

Events proved that the Orkney people were ready for the kind of religion that Haldane brought to them. It would be easy to suggest that his own account of as many as 6000 people attending one of his sermons in the open air must be an exaggeration, but the speed with which everywhere in Orkney the Dissenters organized themselves into congregations and appealed to the Secession Church to send ministers to serve them testifies to an unusually powerful religious revival. A church was built in Kirkwall in 1796, enlarged in 1800, and replaced in 1849. The congregation in Sanday built a church in 1807 only to replace it with a larger one in 1850. Rousay got its church in 1834.[11] Churches were built in the other islands during the same period and were enlarged at surprisingly frequent intervals; on some occasions services had to be held in the fields, the churches not being large enough.[12] After 1874 the membership of the United Presbyterian Church failed to keep pace with the rising population in the nation as a whole, but its progress in Orkney had still to be checked. The *Orkney Herald* reported on 6 September 1875 that in Rousay "the U.P. Church will probably be enlarged next summer as there is hardly room in it for the entire population."

Although he rejected it as an adult, it was probably fortunate for Muir that he grew up within this vigorous movement rather than in the languishing Established Church or the more severe and restrictive Free Church. The difference between the Seceders and the church from which they broke away had at first been strictly limited, but the logic of their position drove the Seceders ultimately into rejecting the influence of the secular world on the spiritual one. Demands for the spiritual independence of the church led inevitably to recognition of the spiritual independence of the individual. Erskine himself, defending his views before a commission appointed by the General Assembly of the Church of Scotland, asserted "the merely administrative nature of all church power" (a sentiment with which Muir would surely have agreed) and "the right of private judgment."[13] Peter Buchan, minister of the Secession congregation in Holm, declared that "in religious matters we are to have no master but Jesus."[14]

Paradoxically, although part of the original impetus of the Secession had been a desire for stricter adherence to Calvinist theology, the United Presbyterian Church evolved into what can be argued was the most liberal and tolerant of the presbyterian sects in Scotland. A twentieth century historian of the U.F. Church is able to write of the U.P. Church: "By a curious irony of fate, a church which had begun in passionate revolt against all theological liberalism, which indeed remained in essentials very orthodox indeed, had been constrained by circumstances to figure as a pioneer movement out of the Calvinistic bondage."[15]

This was the church in which the poet was brought up. One must allow for a degree of formalism and authority in most nineteenth century institutions; but, even by the standards of the twentieth century, the U.P. Church at the time when Muir was a boy cannot be characterized as oppressive either in faith or discipline.

The members of the Free Church, founded in 1843, insisted that their origins lay, not in a "secession", but in a "disruption". The distinction was held to be more than academic. Like the Seceders of more than a century before, the founders of the Free Church sought a stricter theology and an end to lay patronage. Like them they did not set out to found a church but rather to reform the Church of Scotland from within. The failure of the "evangelical" faction to gain control of the General Assembly in 1843 led to the withdrawal of a large body of ministers and elders from the meeting and the announcement of an "Act of Separation". Within a few weeks about a third of the ministers of the Church of Scotland had thrown in their lot with the new body. But only six Orkney ministers (including George Ritchie of Rousay) did so; and this was a significantly smaller proportion than in Scotland as a whole. The influence of the ministers in any parish was crucial. In Rousay 27 elders and deacons signed a declaration in support of the Disruption. The laird was not pleased. He wrote to Robert Scarth: "The Free Church party shows far too much party violence. It is to be hoped that as the angry spirit raised by the secession cools down some moderation will prevail."[16] But Traill's hopes for an early return to moderation were over-sanguine. During the time of his successor as laird the angry spirit of the Free Church, raised first against the spiritual power of the landlords, came to be directed against the secular power of the same landlords, and nowhere more so than in Rousay itself.

The depleted congregation of the Established Church in Rousay was slow to revive. Even forty years later there were difficulties in recruiting new elders: the minister informed the Session in 1886 that none of the five persons nominated by the congregation would accept office.

The allegations made by Haldane against the Established clergy in Orkney were still being made in the second half of the nineteenth century. Robert Scarth seems to have regarded the incompetence and lax morality of ministers of the Established Church in Orkney as so far beyond dispute that he conveyed to the Patronage Committee of the General Assembly his suspicion that the Earl of Zetland's agents (who were members of the Free Church) went out of their way to recommend to the Earl's patronage ministers who were likely to bring the Established Church into disrepute. This speculation cost Scarth one farthing damages for libel in the Court of Session.[17]

Five years after Scarth's libel case he wrote: "I hope to see Edward Gordon introduce and carry easily a Bill for the abolition of Patronage in the Church of Scotland."[18] Scarth's wishes were fulfilled and he could take some satisfaction from having, through the publicity attending the libel action taken against him, helped to bring the issue to a conclusion.

One might have supposed that the removal of the major cause of both the Secession and the Disruption would have brought the three denominations back together. But this did not prove to be the case. The United Presbyterians had long decided that the church should be a voluntary society of believers, while, for its part, the Free Church remained suspicious of the more liberal theology of the other churches. A scheme for the union of the United Presbyterian with the Free Church, first raised in 1863, had been abandoned in 1873; but, in the following year, the two churches joined forces in an attack on the bill to end patronage, and demanded, in the words of the Holm U.P. congregation (which petitioned parliament), "the Disestablishment and disendowment of the Church of Scotland."

The right of patronage (regarded by some as a property right no different from any other, but, because it was held by the Earl of Zetland, not dear to the heart of the Rousay landlord or his factor), the spiritual independence of the church from secular

society, and the retention of Calvinist dogma in its strict form—
these were the live religious issues in the parish of Rousay, as they
were elsewhere in Scotland, when Muir was a boy. How people
felt about them must have been influenced by what they felt about
their local ministers. Each of the three in Rousay was, in his own
way, a distinctive character.

Of the three ministers, the United Presbyterian Mr Pirie, who
came to the island in 1883, seems to have been the best advertisement for organized religion. He described his work in the
*Kirkwall Monthly Messenger* for September 1900:

> The congregation, owing to its "insular" character, has been
> all along a difficult field for religious work. The church is
> built on the Rousay shore, in order to accommodate three
> islands. The members have to cross the sea or the Rousay
> hills for worship, and consequently there can be neither
> concentration of labour nor modern congregational organis-
> ation. Sabbath-schools, Bible classes, prayer meetings, and all
> special services have to be held over the seas and hills in
> classrooms, miles away from the church.[19]

Mr Pirie's admission that there was no room for "modern
congregational organisation" is interesting. Members of U.P.
congregations in the towns enjoyed at that time a comprehensive
social organization based on the church, with meetings and
groups catering for every age-group and section of the congregation. The regular newsletter published by the Kirkwall congregation lists enough activities to occupy the leisure hours of most of
its members, and there must have been powerful social pressures
for all to involve themselves. But the pervasive influence of this
kind of structure could not be brought to bear on the Muir family
in Wyre.

The minister of the Free Church, Alexander M'Callum, was as
controversial and divisive a figure as Mr Pirie was universally
acceptable. Within six months of his appointment there was an
ominous entry in the Session Record (July 1881) to the effect that
he required "a period of rest in which he should be free from the
care and strain of the active duties of the pastorate." It seems that

M'Callum had a drink problem, though several years were to pass before it was brought into the open. Indeed, from the time that he appeared before the Napier Commission, M'Callum was treated by the radical press as something of a folk hero. The *Orkney Herald*, for example, made a great deal of his declaration of a "holy war" against landlords at a speech in Dingwall to the Highland Land Law Reform Association.[20]

The arena in which M'Callum challenged the landlord in his own area was the Rousay School Board. The Board had been constituted in 1873 following the introduction of compulsory schooling under the Education (Scotland) Act 1872. A public meeting had agreed to avoid the expense of an election by appointing to the new Board a group of establishment figures— the three ministers, a farmer, and the landlord. Burroughs, though not actually living in Rousay at the time, was appointed chairman. But this unanimity did not last and, in the first election after the Napier Commission, the Free Church took a foothold which could be exploited through the eagerness of the other members to avoid any unpleasantness. The *Christian Leader* openly gloated at the discomfiture of Burroughs, who held his seat but came third in the poll after James Leonard and M'Callum. The first meeting of the new Board proved a lively one: there was a row over who would lead the meeting in prayer, the Clerk was dismissed, Burroughs resigned in protest, and M'Callum was appointed chairman. The place left vacant by Burroughs' resignation was filled, not by a by-election but by the co-option of a Free Church supporter. The Board then set about the dismissal of all the teachers in the area who were not members of the Free Church, a piece of blatant sectarianism which the *Scotsman* quoted in a plea to have the powers of school boards amended. Those members of the Board, now in a minority, who were not members of the Free Church, found themselves in an uncomfortable position. Mr Craigie of Egilsay, unwilling to be present at the dismissal of two teachers, had to threaten to climb out of the window before M'Callum, who had locked the door to retain a quorum, would permit him to leave. He had earlier offered to resign if the Board would allow his place to be taken by someone acceptable to the people of Egilsay, to which M'Callum had replied that "the appointment rested with the Board and it did not matter whether the people of Egilsay were pleased or otherwise".

The Board eventually consisted entirely of Free Church members, only two of whom had been elected.[21]

What eventually brought an end to the reign of the Free Church was the minister's drink problem. This reached the ears of the Orkney Free Church Presbytery (and, through the courtesy of the *Orcadian*, the public) in 1888; and in January 1889 M'Callum offered his resignation to the Rousay Session, which then, by seven votes to two, made the extraordinary decision to inform the Presbytery that his departure at that time would produce such a state of affairs that would render it impossible for the Free Church to continue on the island. In the event, the congregation did survive his departure though not without the resignation of some of its members. These events occurred in the year of Edwin Muir's baptism.

Alexander Spark, minister of the Established Church in Rousay from 1885 to 1916, was controversial in a slightly different way. From the time of his appointment he showed a marked reluctance to live in his parish. He was censured for this by the Presbytery in 1887 and again in 1888 when it was reported that he was living in Kirkwall and preaching in Rousay only once a month. His popularity in the island may be judged from the fact that in the School Board election of 1895 he came bottom of the poll among ten candidates. (Mr Pirie topped the poll; Mr McLeman, successor to M'Callum at the Free Church, came sixth.)

The reason which Spark gave for his absence from the parish was the poor state of repair of the manse in which he was expected to live. The heritors, who were responsible for the cost of repairs, were always unwilling to spend more than they had to, but they did set about rebuilding the Rousay manse, though not to the standards set by Mr Spark. It seems that he set rather high standards: when his dispute with the heritors reached court in 1888, argument centred round his demand for marble fire-places in his drawing-room and dining-room. The legal arguments smouldered on until a settlement was reached in 1904.

Meanwhile Spark began to live beyond his income, and in 1890 a meeting of his creditors obtained an assignment of his stipend; in 1899 Burroughs' legal adviser in Edinburgh pointed out to him that it was useless to sue Spark for neglect of the manse since he was "more or less bankrupt."[22] Burroughs, at war with the Free

Church and disgusted with the minister of the Established
Church, took to attending worship at the United Presbyterian
Church, he and his wife being henceforth listed annually at the
head of the roll of "Non-communicant members".

So, of the three ministers in the parish, one was power-hungry
and a secret drinker, and the second worldly and extravagant. It
was fortunate for Muir that his minister was the third of them,
Alexander Pirie. The various disputes, which must have been the
talk of the islands when Muir was a boy, were not calculated to
give him a respect for religious institutions.

Anyone who reads the church records and the local newspapers of
the time could be forgiven for supposing that religion in Rousay
amounted to no more than a petty and vindictive struggle for
power among three mutually antagonistic factions. What one has
also to recognize, over and above all the minor troubles, is the
shadow of Calvin. In his biography of John Knox, which consists
very largely of a relentless attack on the character and influence of
the revered Scottish reformer, Muir seems to unleash his anger
against an evil that was still casting its shadow when the
nineteenth century was drawing to an end. He acknowledged
afterwards that it was not a good book. Knox had been too near
him for comfort: "He was still too close for me to see him clearly,
for I had met him, or someone very like him, over and over, it
seemed to me, in the course of my life."[23] Nevertheless, it was
probably a book that Muir needed to write.

It was Knox who had brought to Scotland what Muir calls "the
extraordinary doctrines" developed by Calvin at Geneva.[24] The
particularly extraordinary element in these doctrines was the
belief in election—the belief that God, for reasons beyond the
understanding of men, has, from all eternity, chosen some men to
live for ever, and others to perish. Its classic Scottish statement is
to be found in chapter three of the Westminster Confession of
1560:

> By the decrees of God, for the manifestation of His glory,
> some men and angels are predestined unto everlasting life,
> and others foreordained to everlasting death. These angels
> and men thus predestined and foreordained, are particularly

  and unchangeably designed, and their number is so certain
  and definite, that it cannot be either increased or diminished.

This statement, though under challenge, was known and understood 300 years after its composition. The good-natured Mr Pirie,
the dictatorial Mr M'Callum, and the worldly Mr Spark all had
signified their assent to it at their ordination. It was what their
denominations had in common. The Muir family and all their
neighbours were familiar with it. They would not challenge it
openly.
  Muir found the doctrine repugnant. Some of his early work
shows his distaste at the idea of a cruel and arbitrary god. *The
Three Brothers* contains (at the expense of the pace of the
narrative) long passages of debate between the Calvinists and the
Anabaptists. *Variations on a Time Theme* shows awareness of the
futility of life if its outcome is already ordained. Does our way end
"at the dead centre of the boundless plain"? If so, it is, thinks
Muir, "a sad stationary journey". The word "Time" is used in a
curious way in this poem, for it refers, not to a sequence of
passing events, but to something that goes on for ever and yet is
not eternity. Is not "Time" to be identified with Calvinist
predestination? Christ and men are joined in the poem as victims
of "Time":

> Summoned, elected, armed and crowned by Time,
> Tried and condemned, stripped and disowned by
>     Time;
> Suckled and weaned, plumped and full-fed by Time,
> Defrauded, starved, physicked and bled by Time;
> Buried alive and buried dead by Time.

These lines refer, in the first place, to the life of Christ, who
withdrew from eternity to live in Time. But they apply also to
mankind as a whole, because Christ and men have been defrauded
and set at nothing if Time has already trapped them:

> If there's no power can burst the rock of Time,
> No rescuer from the dungeon stock of Time,
> Nothing in earth or heaven to set us free:
> Imprisonment's for ever; we're the mock of Time,
> While lost and empty lies Eternity.

There is bitterness here. The Calvinist certainty that the number to be saved is arbitrarily fixed may point to an empty eternity: the number fixed may be nil.

Along with the soul-searching about Calvinism there appears in some of the early poems a thoughtful criticism of the effect of Calvinism on society. The society in which Muir had been brought up was one in which Calvin and Knox were held to be above open criticism. He discovered as an adult that these national heroes had feet of clay and he wrote of the "accustomed unction" of Knox's standard biographer, Dr M'Crie. Muir's own biography of Knox was "written for the purpose of making some breach in the enormous reverence in which Knox has been held and is still held in Scotland, a reverence which I had to fight with too in my early days."[25]

What Muir found particularly repugnant in Calvinism was what he saw as its cult of violence. The Calvinist, he suggested in a letter to Herbert Read, saw "a divine principle in wrath".[26] The logic of the Calvinist position was that, if God's judgments really were arbitrary, "then the moral judgments of his elect would tend to acquire the same qualities."[27] In an incident in a Glasgow street, in which one man beat another and explained, "I ken he hasna hurt me, but I'm gaun tae hurt him!", Muir detected "a sordid image of fate as Calvin saw it."[28]

In the same way that the logic of predestination justifies man's cruelty to man, it justifies also the harsh cruelty of fate. Sandy, in *The Three Brothers*, calls such things as the plague and drownings at sea, "God's arrangement". But Muir, who had some experience of these arrangements, did not take refuge in such faith. His sympathies lie with the Anabaptist, Boyle, who says: "That's like the Calvinists! They fasten on something especially awful and call it the invention of God, and think what braw folk they are to worship a God that's as terrible as that."[29]

There were those only too anxious to serve such a terrible God. The policy of the Scottish Church in the past was, according to Muir, "a policy of espionage and repression".[30] The spirit of this policy was sufficiently close to Muir for him to feel some affinity with the world drawn by Kafka and for him to write a poem like "The Interrogation". In *Scottish Journey* he expresses the belief that secret drinking was partly the result of "the past discipline of presbyterianism, whose foundation was a universal vigilance: the function of the elders having been to keep a strict watch on the congregation and the minister, of the congregation to dog the steps of the minister and the elders, and of the minister to have his eye on everyone."[31]

Secret drinking was, if one excepts the case of the Free Church minister, probably not a problem among the inhabitants of Rousay, Egilsay and Wyre. There are few references to intemperance among the records of the kirk sessions. What the records do indicate is that fornication was a more popular activity; their weekly accounts of penances given to offenders make tedious reading. The penances were evidently not very effective. Muir comments: "To describe the sordid and general tyranny which this fearful institution wielded for over two hundred years would be wearisome and would take too long. It is only necessary to say that the time-honoured Scottish tradition of fornication triumphantly survived all its terrors."[32] In Muir's day sinners were no longer required to do public penance, but in all three congregations in Rousay they were required to appear before the Session, and their names were faithfully recorded. One effect of the procedure was to bring the social pressure of the Church to bear on prospective fathers, and the name of many a man admonished by the Session appears later in the record as an elder. In some ways the procedure was part of the ritual of growing up; sin, marriage, and membership of the Church being associated with one another:

> George and Mrs George Stevenson having applied for admission to the fellowship they were admitted after having been rebuked for the sin of ante-nuptial fornication.
>
> *Rousay U.P. Record, 3 November 1894*

For some reason, Muir's cousin, Sutherland, who lived with the family in Wyre, and who was the father of a number of illegitimate children, escaped all these pressures and never married. His lecherous nocturnal tours were not an invention of his own. A report issued in 1884 by the Committee on Morals of the Orkney Synod complained of "loose and debasing practices which are said to prevail among unsanctified persons in some part of Orkney. Those hours of the night during which they ought to be quietly resting in their beds, they spend prowling about in the darkness, or receiving indecent visits from persons who do so."

Many years later, Muir derived some wry, if affectionate, amusement from both Sutherland and the Church by sending the unsanctified Sutherland to heaven:

> Am I here
> Because I duly read the Bible on Sundays
> And drowsed through the minister's sermon? I know
>     my duty.
> But in the evening.
> I led the young lads to the orra lasses
> Across the sound to the other islands.
>
> *There's Nothing Here*

The probability is that the great majority of the inhabitants of Wyre would have shared Sutherland's attitudes while deploring his behaviour. They would do their duty on Sunday and see no contradiction between that and their activities during the rest of the week. The Kirk Session Records show that the Session still maintained its right to examine the lives of the members of the congregation and that this was accepted as the price of member-ship; but the Session could no longer dominate their lives. Apart from anything else, there were now three rival churches. Mem-bers could, and did, move from one to another, sometimes for reasons which worried the Committee on Morals:

> It is a reproach to any congregation if it readily admits fugi-tives from discipline, who come with tarnished character from other congregations so as to escape from being faithfully dealt with by them.

The concern expressed shows that such things did happen. In the competition for members the price of admission was being lowered.

Even in the matter of sleeping through the weekly sermon, the power of the Kirk Session was slipping away. At the time that the Muir family were members of the Holm United Presbyterian Congregation, the Session resolved to do something about poor attendance:

> After conversation with regard to the non-attendance or
> irregular attendance of certain parties at public worship on
> the Lord's day the elders present agreed to between them call
> on the parties and try to get matters remedied.

This is hardly the language of a group conscious of its own power.
The Muir family were not good attenders, but the only sanction
that could be applied to them was a friendly, and probably
embarrassed, visit from their elder. Such visits were unlikely to
produce any result. When a family in Rousay were reported to the
Free Church Session for non-attendance at worship, they were
visited by the minister on no fewer than three occasions before the
Session resolved that it "would be inexpedient to prosecute the
matter."

Muir insisted that he had known John Knox, or someone like
him, all his life. But the John Knox that Muir knew was a ghost of
his former self. By 1890 the weakening of the Kirk Session's
power of persuasion must have been obvious to all.

A significant number of Church of Scotland ministers had begun
quietly to abandon the tenets of Calvinism during the eighteenth
century. They still had to go through the formality of giving their
assent to the Westminster Confession on their ordination (though
in 1766 one young man, more daring or more honest than most,
added the words "erroribus exceptis" after his signature, and was
not challenged). Both the Secession of the eighteenth century and
the Disruption of the nineteenth were reactions to such "moderate" views, but there was more to the new denominations than a
desire to return to the stricter theology of an earlier age. To a
considerable extent they were setting their face against dis-
honesty; and there is a historical inevitability, associated with the
Romantic Movement, in their rejection of the confident rational-
ism of the "moderate" majority in the Church of Scotland. The
rationalist outlook produced a poet like James Thomson: it took
the background of theological assertion and speculation of the
United Presbyterian Church to produce a poet like Muir. The
arid logic of Calvinism did have behind it an awareness of the
eternal. This was what the United Presbyterian Church had to
offer Muir. What it lacked was a convincing explanation of the

relationship between the eternal and the temporal, and this Muir had to find for himself.

The "moderate" outlook had little to do with tolerance. When a young minister, John Macleod Campbell, offered an alternative to Calvinism by proclaiming that Christ died for all men, he was hounded from the Church of Scotland. At his trial before the General Assembly in 1831 men who did not themselves believe in Calvinism quoted the Westminster Confession at him. Campbell went on to prove himself the greatest Scottish theologian of the age in a series of books, of which *The Nature of the Atonement* is the best known. What distinguishes him above all else is his honesty. "The constraint felt in preaching Christ to all, while believing that He only died for some." he writes, "is easily understood." It was not easily understood by the General Assembly. As one of his opponents candidly stated at his trial, "It is by the Confession of Faith that we must stand: by it we hold our livings."[33]

The dominance of Calvinist thought was so strong that even Campbell himself tried to show that his assertion of God's love for all men was consistent with the Westminster Confession. Yet, within a decade of Campbell's expulsion from the Established Church, the Secession Church had its own arch-heretic, James Morison, who assaulted Calvinism head on. "It is," he wrote, "a creed for tyrants. It is a creed for all who would wish an excuse to tread the masses of mankind underfoot."[34] Morison attracted many followers, some of whom travelled to Orkney to reason with their brethren in the Secession Church. "They denounced Calvinism as one of the most hideous and unscriptural systems that had ever been formulated by man, and held it forth as utterly inconsistent with a free gospel," wrote David Webster, who was the Muirs' minister in Kirkwall.[35]

There was no more room for Morison in the Secession and United Presbyterian Churches than there had been for Campbell in the Established Church, but in the course of the nineteenth century the will to uphold the doctrines of Calvin was weakening in all three Presbyterian Churches. In 1879 the United Presbyterian Church adopted a Declaratory Act which effectively dropped the Westminster Confession as a statement of faith. Even in the Free Church there were moves to reject the doctrines of the Confession, an amending motion being carried in 1889.

Muir, then, was born at the very time that the churches were
rejecting their Calvinist heritage, even though official spokesmen
felt obliged to reconcile new beliefs with the old. That such
reconciliation demanded a certain amount of tortuous word-play,
rather on a par with the unctiousness for which Muir criticised Dr
M'Crie, did not add anything to the credibility of churchmen.

The theological speculation of the time would hardly have
made much direct impact on the young Muir, though the debates
of the Synod in Edinburgh are certain to have been a matter for
discussion among the adult members of the Rousay congregation.
Muir would have been more aware of three tendencies at the local
level which were helping to weaken the hold of Calvinism. These
were: the growth of radical political thought within the Church,
the fashion for religious revivals, and the fact that, even after
three centuries of Calvinist Presbyterianism, pre-Reformation
and even pre-Christian modes of thought were still to be found.

The demand for a responsible social order in which there was
adequate provision for the poor did not in itself conflict with
Calvinist tradition, and it can be argued that the presbyterian
form of government, in which elders and ministers were elected
by the people, was favourable to the growth of democracy; yet, in
the long term, the kind of radical thought that encouraged the
recognition of the individual's right to make his own judgments
was inimical to the moral paternalism exercised by all three
Presbyterian denominations in Scotland.

It had been assumed from the time of the Reformation that the
minister would play a social role in the parish. When, in 1844, a
new minister was being sought by the Established Church in
Rousay to replace George Ritchie on his defection to the Free
Church, George William Traill wrote to Robert Scarth: "I trust
we shall get a good active man zealous for the Temporal welfare of
his parishioners as well as for their moral and religious improvement."[36] There is no reason to doubt Traill's sincerity, but of
course the landlord's view of what was their temporal welfare was
not necessarily the same as their own.

Landlords could, as a rule, depend on the support of the clergy
of the Established Church. Donald MacLeod, in his recollections
of the Sutherland clearances, recorded that "the oppressors
always appealed to them for sanction and justification and were

not disappointed."[37] The evictions in Rousay of 1845-1848 were roundly condemned by George Ritchie, who warned Traill that "the Earth is the Lord's and the fullness thereof."[38] But by that time Ritchie had already joined the Free Church and his political outlook may have been partly the reason. There is no doubt that part of the attraction of religious dissent was political. Drummond and Bulloch suggest that the demand for the popular election of ministers, a continual theme for a century and a half, was not so exclusively religious as the evangelicals claimed: it was part of a middle-class demand for more local power.

It was characteristic of ministers both of the Free Church and of the Secession Church to oppose landlords. Mr M'Callum challenged the landlord at the hearing of the Napier Commission, he fought him on the School Board, and he proclaimed at a Land Law Reform Association conference that "the voice of the Church of God ought not to be silent, but should be clearly heard in the pleadings of this righteous cause."[39] When, to the laird's consternation, Rousay was declared a crofting parish (and thus subject to the Act), M'Callum held a thanksgiving service.[40]

The Free Church, perhaps because of its middle-class membership and the social background of its ministers, did not in the end identify itself with hostility to property rights; but its association with the Liberal Party was marked, as was that of the United Presbyterian Church. An analysis of the voting of ministers in the general election of 1868 shows that 1221 Church of Scotland ministers voted Conservative, and 67 Liberal; 33 Free Church ministers voted Conservative, and 607 Liberal. The figures for the United Presbyterian ministers are even more striking: only one voted Conservative, and 474 Liberal.[41] In the same election of 1868 the Rev. Neil Rose rounded up votes in Rousay for the Liberal candidate, much to the annoyance of the factor, who encouraged one of the farmers to warn voters, "Mind your leases."[42] The *Edinburgh Courant* denounced Rose's intervention and complained that "in Orkney and Shetland this kind of drumming of their flocks by the clergy was almost universal."[43]

Religion itself had a party political tinge, the three denominations being regarded for some purposes as parties. In 1888 a local newspaper, in publishing the names of candidates in School Board elections, gave also, not the political party, but the religious denomination of each of them.

No one would guess from Muir's writings that he had been brought up in a place where religion and politics were so interwoven. The moderate socialism to which he inclined most of his life is not associated in any way with his religious upbringing. He thought of Calvinism as appealing particularly to "the merchant and banking classes, the progenitors of modern Capitalism."[44] What his book on Knox does not take account of is the decline of Calvinism in the face of reforming political and social attitudes within the Church itself: he saw it only as a system which had been deserted by its worshippers. Either Muir did not recognize the changed Calvinism of his boyhood world or he did not attach much importance to it in comparison with the Calvinism of the past. The Knox that he claimed to know from his own past is to a considerable extent a reconstruction of a figure from an earlier age.

The second feature of the Church that helped to undermine the foundations of Calvinism in Muir's early years was the fashion for religious revivals. This was something that Muir did recognize, though he did not see it as hostile to the spirit of Calvinism. He seems rather to have regarded it with some embarrassment, which is the attitude of someone directly affected by it.

Moody, the American revivalist, visited Scotland in 1859, and for a while afterwards revivals periodically swept as far as Orkney. The kind of salvation preached by Moody was one which was open to all who repented of their sins. Amid the emotional fervour of revivalist meetings the doctrine of predestination had no place. How could it? John Macleod Campbell had already remarked on the difficulty of preaching conversion to sinners while at the same time telling them that God had already chosen, on quite arbitrary grounds, the saved from the damned. The churches offered no resistance to the revivalist movement, the Free Church in particular succumbing to the new emotion and sense of personal commitment. The United Presbyterian Church had less need of revivals, since, as Webster points out, there had been "more or less a religious awakening over the islands" ever since the Secession Church had first reached Orkney.[45] Muir recalls that a revivalist who did preach in Webster's church in Kirkwall made few converts, for the people "refused to be chaffed into salvation". But when he was 14 Muir attended some outdoor services and

consented to be "saved".[46] The ambivalent attitude of his parents
to his conversion may have been typical of members of their
Church. They were glad he was starting to take religion seriously
but doubtful of the virtue of revivals.

Yet the revivals did help to liberate people from the Calvinist
system. A religion that set out to offer people an individual choice
of action could never return to the doctrine of predestination.

The third way in which the Calvinist grip was loosened lay in the
continuation of older beliefs that resisted the system. Eliade has
commended the study of the folklore of peasant communities in
Europe for the understanding of primitive religion because of the
way in which archaic features survive in the Christian beliefs of
these communities. Davidson reminds us that, since the period
during which North European man lived by hunting has to be
measured, not in centuries, but in millenia, "the religious beliefs
of this vast period must have etched themselves deeply into his
mind and spirit."[47] It would be surprising if either the priests of
the Catholic Church or the Presbyterian ministers had entirely
succeeded in eradicating all the traditional beliefs of a conservative people.

All the indications are that, before the coming of the Seceders
to Orkney in the last decade of the eighteenth century, Orkney
ministers did not trouble their flocks much, and could have made
little impression on their fundamental beliefs. It is not to be
wondered at that the Rev. George Barry recognized in his history
in Orkney, published in 1805, the open continuation of religious
practices that had nothing to do with Calvinism:

> To many of the old places of worship, therefore, especially
> such as have been dedicated to particular favourite saints,
> they still pay much veneration, visiting them frequently,
> when they are serious, melancholy, or in a devout mood,
> repeating within their ruinous walls, prayers, paternosters,
> and forms of words of which they have little knowledge.[48]

Other practices had little to do with Christianity at all. The Rev.
John Anderson of Stronsay was thankful that his parishioners
believed in fairies rather than in the ideas of the French Revolution. Half a century later, the Rev. Charles Clouston, more

optimistically, announced that "the light of knowledge is fast chasing away from Orkney the superstitious phantoms of former ignorance." Clouston's optimism was not entirely well-founded. At the time he was writing, Beltane fires ("La Bel Teine"), lit in honour of a Celtic deity, were lit every year in Rousay and accompanied by traditional rituals, despite the disapproval of the Church. And, according to the reminiscences of John Firth, as late as 1887 (the year of Muir's birth) people still believed in the malicious tricks of the fairies at the time of births and deaths. The indications are that a character in one of Dennison's stories is not exaggerating when he says: "People here live in mortal terror of invasion from the spirit world."[49]

The way in which these beliefs continued incongruously along-side those of the church is described in John D. Mackay's memories of his boyhood in Papa Westray:

> Family worship was conducted in most households with the utmost devotion and hard and fast lines were drawn between conduct which would qualify for Heavenly bliss, or for eternal damnation. Grace was said before, and sometimes after, every meal, and, with the declining power of the Laird, the prestige of the minister was enhanced. Weighty discourses on the nature of life after death could be heard whenever two or three islanders met together, but the conversation might, at any time, be switched over to the Little Grey People who lived on the North Hill and their latest escapades.[50]

The incongruities were sometimes apparent only in retrospect. A lady confessed to Ernest Marwick, "It seems strange to me now that grannie who was such a good living woman and read her bible every day without fail could talk about fairies and the like and I have the feeling she believed in them.[51]

Pagan beliefs were paraded before the minister himself, so that "while the clergyman was waiting to give the body Christian burial, the bearers of the coffin were turning it carefully at the side of the grave in consonance with the course of the sun."[52] Their action is a telling symbol and a reminder that Calvinism may have been a great deal less firmly established than its adherents cared to admit or than Muir indicates in *An Autobiography* and *John Knox*.

That Calvinism was on the decline in Orkney during Muir's boyhood does not change the fact that, for the greater part of his life, Muir saw Christianity largely in terms prescribed by the Calvinist tradition. His liberation from this version of Christianity did not come within the Presbyterian Church. So far as Muir was concerned, the reforms instituted in the United Presbyterian Church during the last three decades of the nineteenth century were largely wasted effort. His view of the Church was strongly coloured by his awareness of history and tradition. He was, one must assume, too honest to come to terms with the contradictions of current theology through the kind of intellectual ingenuity adopted by many of the more thinking members of his Church; and he was of too speculative a turn of mind to accept doctrine instinctively in the way his cousin Sutherland did.

Muir's liberation from Calvinism and his willingness to look afresh at Christianity came through contact with a different kind of attitude to religion from the one he had known as a boy:

I discovered in Italy that Christ had walked on earth.[53]

He had discovered ("discovered" is not too strong a word) the Incarnation.

His letters show that, from 1939, he began to think about life after death. But it was in Italy after the Second World War that the presence everywhere of religious images impressed the fact of the Incarnation on him. The physical presence of the spiritual was not known in Orkney. There he had been aware of religion "chiefly as the sacred word, and the church itself, severe and decent, with its touching bareness and austerity, seemed to cut off religion from the rest of life and from all the week-day world, as if it were a quite specific thing shut within itself, almost jealously by its white-washed walls, furnished with its bare brown varnished benches unlike any other in the whole world, and filled with the odour of ancient Bibles. It did not tell me by any outward sign that the Word had been made flesh."[54]

The outward sign is necessary to the poet. Ultimately, it was for its rejection of the image, of the Incarnation in its fullest sense, that Muir found the Church of his youth wanting. He saw its faith as one of abstraction and rejection of life:

The Word made flesh is here made word again,
A word made word in flourish and arrogant crook.
See there King Calvin with his iron pen,
And God three angry letters in a book.
*The Incarnate One*

This is a powerful condemnation. Is it fair? Is it fair, that is, as a contemporary statement? Few would deny its validity as a picture of Scottish religion of the sixteenth century; but Muir paints with a brush so broad as to cover the nineteenth century as well; neither here nor elsewhere in his work does he show much awareness of change in religious life and attitudes. Yet the religious outlook in Scotland, and in Orkney, had changed, or was changing, during the period of Muir's upbringing, but much of the change was disguised by psychological and historical constraints, notably a continuing reverence for the memory of John Knox and the significance of the Westminster Confession. This disguise encourages Muir to conflate the centuries. Such conflation, besides being natural to his way of thought, suits his artistic purpose, which is to set the image against the abstraction, the Word against the word.

Muir's approach finds justification in the comparative failure, even of the United Presbyterian Church, which was the most adaptable of the three, to break free of its sixteenth century legacy. That legacy was acceptable to those who were happy with the view of Scottish history presented, for example, in Howie's *The Scots Worthies*, a book which, as Muir says, was at one time found in every Scottish farmhouse; but it would hardly satisfy the poet, to whom it gave, "no conception of the splendour of Christendom."[55] In places like Melrose Abbey and the Cathedral at St Andrews he saw traces of something that "symbolised a whole way of life, which was not Catholicism merely, but something which rose under Catholicism."[56] There were traces of it in Orkney too, most obviously in the romanesque cathedral of St Magnus in Kirkwall. But most churches in Orkney had little to show of the achievements of Christendom. R. Menzies Fergusson wrote in 1883: "It is to be regretted that the churches in Orkney are so wanting in tasteful architecture. The principle adopted in their construction seems to have been that of uncouthness, for they are built as nearly as possible to resemble huge barns."[57]

The services which were conducted in these churches paid as little attention to the arts of mankind as did the buildings themselves. Ployen, who visited both Orkney and the mainland of Scotland, was struck by the fact that Scottish religious practice was even more divorced from the finer things of life than that of the Faroes: "Our church ceremonies are sufficiently cold, and adddressed to the reason, to the exclusion of the senses; but the Scottish people have contrived to make their whole worship of God still more frigid than ours, admitting neither altar, altarpiece, lights or organ."[58] Contemporary observations on the character of worship in Orkney churches are hard to come by. Most commentators, including Muir himself, confine themselves to the sermon. Perhaps that is comment enough.

It is fair to add, however, that there was an interest in improving the musical contribution to the services. The strict rule since the Reformation had been that only the Scriptures should be read or sung in church, and this permitted the singing of psalms but not of hymns. The use of musical instruments was entirely forbidden. The Relief Church was the first to break with this tradition by introducing a hymn book in 1794, long before any of its rivals. The Secession Church followed; and, when these two Churches joined to form the United Presbyterian Church, one of the first acts of the new body was to produce a hymn book. This 1851 book was replaced by another, the *Presbyterian Hymnal*, in 1877. This collection, which drew on a wide variety of sources, ancient and modern, Catholic and Protestant, represented a considerable advance over the earlier volume. This was the hymn book that Muir knew. It can by no means be thought of as narrow or Calvinistic. The Church of Scotland and the Free Church introduced hymn books in 1870 and 1873 respectively; but it was only in 1890, following M'Callum's departure, that hymn books were used in Rousay Free Church.

Instrumental music took rather longer to introduce, and, indeed, there was no organ in the Rousay United Presbyterian Church until the year that the Muir family left the area. The first organ to be heard in any Scottish Presbayterian church was in 1863 in Edinburgh. In Orkney it was the Established Church in Rousay that led the way. The *Orkney Herald* of 21 March 1875 reported that the Rousay congregation had introduced a harmonium, a novelty unknown elsewhere in Orkney. It took 20 years for their neighbours in the United Presbyterian Church to follow their example.

The heart of Presbyterian worship was never music or ceremony but remained "the preaching of the Word". It was an exercise that enjoyed a reputation for intellectualism. One of Orkney's Church of Scotland ministers at the time of the Disruption felt compelled to admit that it had been "the practice for congregations to expect, and ministers to furnish, an intellectual treat, instead of the simple teaching of Scripture truths."[59] As Ernest Marwick remembered, those who attended the services of the Free Church gloried in spiritual logic but seldom encountered the numinous: the sermons were essentially a literary exercise.[60]

Whatever the skills of the preacher, the message alone was of little value to the poet, for the poet needed the image. Muir recognized the danger to poetry of the imageless theology in which he grew up; and he wrote to Ernest Marwick of his concern for their mutual friend, Robert Rendall, who combined writing poetry with producing theological works: "I have never been able to understand how Robert manages to reconcile his true intelligence and sensibility with his religious ideas. It is a mystery which must have its roots in his childhood and ancestry. Encourage him, if you can, to write poetry instead of theology."[61] He had escaped that kind of danger.

Living in Rome while serving with the British Council gave Muir the stimulus to relate the poetic image to the historical fact of the Incarnation. By being born on earth as man, God not only sanctified the things of earth, but gave divine sanction to their use as signs of the eternal. What more could a poet wish for? The difficulty of relating man's life on earth to his eternal destiny, a difficulty which the harsh logic of Calvinism gave no answer to, is resolved in a moment by an image, on a wall in Rome, of the meeting of Gabriel and Mary:

> See, they have come together, see,
> While the destroying minutes flow,
> Each reflects the other's face
> Till heaven in hers and earth in his
> Shine steady there.

*The Annunciation*

The Incarnation brings together this world and the next in a
matrix on which is written, not sin, but love. "A religion that
dared to show forth such a mystery for everyone to see would
have shocked the congregation of the north," he thought.[62]

In *The Three Brothers*, David, with only Calvinism as an
unreliable guide, asks, "If there's a God, why doesna he tell us,
why doesna He guide us? I wouldna leave a dog in the state he
leaves us in."[63] The answer to David's question was on a wall in
Rome all the time. It was an answer that corresponded to Muir's
hopes:

> some day
> I know I shall find a man who has done good
> His long lifelong and is
> Image of man from whom all have diverged.
>
> *The Journey Back*

## Chapter Nine

# SCHOOL

IN THE summer of 1901 Mrs Burroughs presented prizes at Kirkwall Burgh School. At the ceremony the provost of Kirkwall consoled those scholars who were not receiving prizes with the thought that "the dunce in education sometimes becomes the profound thinker in later life."[1] Among those present was probably the fourteen year old Edwin Muir, though he was not one of the prize winners. We know that he was a dunce because one of Her Majesty's Inspectors of Schools said so.[2] A few years after Muir's death there was some talk of naming a school in Kirkwall after him. Willa Muir was pleased when this idea came to nothing. "He was not much addicted to schooling when he was a boy in Orkney, was he?" she wrote to Ernest Marwick.[3] Muir hated the school in Wyre and hated the school in Kirkwall only slightly less. Even as an adult he was never able to look on St Magnus Cathedral with an untroubled eye because it was "associated with those mornings when I looked down on Kirkwall, where, hidden among houses, stood the school."[4]

Muir was caught up in an educational system which had been devised only six years before he was born. The Education (Scotland) Act 1872 introduced the principle of education for all and provided arrangements for building schools, appointing teachers, and inspecting the instruction. The energies of those responsible for Scottish education were for many years to come directed towards making the Act work. Their priorities were to provide enough accommodation, to ensure the maximum attendance of pupils, to remove unsatisfactory teachers from office, and to establish minimum standards of attainment for children who were destined to become farm workers, artisans and clerks. It was an adequate preparation for the kind of job in which Muir found himself on leaving school. It left little room for the development of the child as an individual: that was something the child must see to for himself.

Although there was no shortage of good will towards education in Orkney, the new school boards faced immediate practical problems which greatly outweighed any theoretical considerations about the nature of education. New buildings were urgently required and the school boards were enthusiastic about providing them since the cost was to be met by central government. There was less enthusiasm in the school boards for carrying out their own responsibility for getting rid of the considerable legacy of unsatisfactory teachers inherited from the parochial schools.

We have a valuable, comprehensive evaluation of the situation in Orkney in 1873 in the form of a report by George Ramsay, Professor of Humanities at Glasgow University. In August 1873 Ramsay, who had been commissioned by the Board of Education for Scotland to advise on the educational needs of Orkney and Shetland, visited almost every island in Orkney. His report was a frank one. He wrote to his masters of "the wretched condition of the greater part of the school buildings", and gave details of "damp mud floors... walls green with wet... chimneys that will not vent, windows that will not open." The problem of such schools was, in the main, readily solved, for public money was available to replace them. But the problem of very small schools, where the number of pupils was too small to attract enough grant to pay the teachers, required more drastic solutions. "There can be no doubt," Ramsay wrote, "that the system of having a large number of small ill-found schools is expensive, wasteful and inefficient." He suggested that schools with under 50 pupils should be combined with neighbouring schools; but he recognized that certain isolated schools, including Wyre with its sixteen pupils, could never be combined with any other school.[5]

Rousay School Board, very much concerned with the peculiar difficulties of its area, sought and obtained a private meeting with Ramsay in September 1873. The professor showed reluctance to agree to the provision of schools in Wyre and Egilsay—he felt that the children should be boarded in other islands—but, according to the Board's record of the meeting, finally agreed to recommend the payment of the additional grant which would make it possible to run the two schools.[6] For its part, the Board undertook to use its "utmost exertions" to obtain a school for Wyre and, immediately following its meeting with Professor Ramsay, obtained from General Burroughs a site for a school on the farm of the Bu.

With the building of the school in Wyre the Board's problems were only beginning. Both Lord Napier and Professor Ramsay had urged the educational advantages of appointing women as teachers in small schools.[7] Ignoring the educational arguments, the Rousay Board, which had appointed men to every other position it had to offer, advertised for an unqualified female teacher for Wyre in the hope of providing education there on the cheap. For the next twenty years the island saw a succession of poorly paid and poorly qualified teachers. Such minutes that survive show that the Board had to discuss the latest crisis in Wyre every few months. The problem was that the Board was not prepared to pay the same salaries in Wyre as it did in Rousay. The Board thought, or affected to think, that the problem of keeping teachers stemmed from the practice of other boards in Orkney tempting away its teachers. Several letters in the *Orcadian* in November 1890 drew attention to the high-handed way in which the Rousay Board treated its teachers, and one of the correspondents, while admitting that the woman teacher in Wyre was probably overpaid, complained that the harshness of the Board could be seen in the fact that Wyre had had four teachers in five years.

Parents were, in any case, less than totally enthusiastic about sending their children to school. In many people's eyes schooling was a fit activity for the winter only, when there was not enough work on the land to demand the presence of children. The 1872 Act required the attendance of children at school, but nobody expected compulsion to be effective. More than twenty years after the passing of the Act H.M. Inspector of Schools for Orkney complained that children were often away from school throughout the summer months.[8] Muir himself did not attend school until he was seven years old but this was because of poor health. In Kirkwall, health, weather and distance all kept him from being a regular attender; and even his sympathetic father sometimes needed him at home to herd the cows.[9]

Given all the difficulties, it is surprising that Orkney children got as good an education as they did. Even as early as 1842, when the only schools were the parochial schools of the Church of Scotland, the New Statistical Account estimated that only 62 people out of a total population in Rousay, Egilsay and Wyre of 1262 were unable to read.

The theories of those now in charge of education were, in some ways, remarkably modern sounding. The "Regulations for the Management of Schools", issued in 1891 by the South Ronaldsay School Board, stipulate, for example, that "teachers must treat all scholars with absolute impartiality, and must not make use of threats, taunts, or ridicule, so as to destroy the legitimate confidence and self-respect of scholars."[10] General Burroughs' views on education, as given to the scholars of Wasbister School in 1881, have an enlightened ring: "You will come to school to be taught how to learn to educate yourselves."[11] But a report of a discussion in Orkney County Council puts his views in a different light: "General Burroughs said Drawing was not required in a county such as Orkney. What was required was tuition in agriculture, fishing, domestic hygiene, domestic economy, darning, sewing, and cooking."[12] The General was, it seems, an early advocate of "relevance" in education: he saw no place in Orkney for art, nor (presumably) for poetry.

The Wyre school seems to have got off to a good start after the 1872 Act. It was taught, according to H.M. Inspector in 1876, "with great care and judgement."[13] A year later it was said that "order and general tone leave nothing to be desired." The Inspector in 1884 reported that "the children are frank, honest and eager." It should not be thought that these reports were made by Inspectors who were unwilling to offend. The report for the year 1885 removed any doubt about their frankness: "New maps are required. The condition of the school is not very satisfactory. Geography and History do not meet the requirements. Copy writing is very careless. Sewing is very fair. There has been a change of teacher since my last visit." There were many changes of teacher in the years immediately before Muir started school. But Muir was evidently lucky. His teacher, Miss Angus, got a good report in 1894, the year that he started school; she was particularly commended for "the excellent training in sentence construction", a feature of the school that must deserve at least a little of the credit for the lucid prose style that Muir developed.

The Inspector may have liked the school but Edwin Muir did not. "I disliked school from the start", he wrote; and he claimed to have been good at nothing but singing. In his autobiography he pictures school (whether from genuine memory or unconsciously

under the influence of Wordworth, it is impossible to say) as a
prison from which there was no escape: he was "flung" into it and
it gave him "a feeling of being shut in some narrow, clean,
wooden place."¹⁴ This description carries the image of the coffin
as much as of the prison. Going to school marked the death of
what he thought of as his real childhood.

The symbolic landscape of Muir's poems is characteristically
one of open space. The scene is almost invariably an outdoor one.
When it is confined in any way, within a building, a wood, a
"narrow place", the effect is claustrophobic. One thinks of the
"tall and echoing passages of the labyrinth" the "deadly wood" (of
"The City"), the "drugged thicket" (of "The Grove"), the "room
in a place where no doors open" (of "The Refugees Born for a
Land Unknown"), and of

> The poor ghost of Euridice
> Still sitting in her silver chair,
> Alone in Hades' empty hall.
>
> *Orpheus' Dream*

Sunshine is the sign of freedom, darkness that of imprisonment.
Milton was "shut in his darkness", though what he saw in his
mind's eye was outside—"the fields of paradise". Paradise is out
of doors, as was Eden.

The windows of the Wyre classroom were too high to allow a
view of the outside world; inside the room "time moved by
minute degrees" and the schoolboy would sit "invisibly pushing
the hands of the clock" and then "waken to realize that they had
scarcely moved."¹⁵ The memory of that first experience of school
contributed something to the image that appears in

> He watched upon the floor
> The punctual minutes crawl
> Towards the remaining wall
> Into eternity.
>
> *Effigies*

The trouble with school was not that the teacher was cruel, but
that school was not home. The three brothers in Muir's novel
started school, and

When they returned in the evening Falsyth was strange to
them, and they seemed to have been a long time away; and
they ran round the outbuildings, looking into the byre, the
stable, the barn, as if the house were no longer their home,
and their real life were elsewhere.[16]

This is how going to school must have seemed to Muir. It marked
the end of that special relationship with the Bu that is lovingly
described in *An Autobiography*. The reality of his childhood is
remembered, not as the clean wooden place which one day made
him so sick that the teacher had to take him outside and let him sit
in "a grassy field",[17] but as "the sunny hill" above the Bu.[18]

Despite the clock, Edwin Muir's time at the Wyre school was
brief. When he was eight years old his family moved to the farm
of Garth, near Kirkwall. He was admitted to Kirkwall Burgh
School on 9 January 1896.[19] His first day at school and his
interview with the slightly intimidating headmaster, Mr McEwen,
are recounted in convincing detail in his autobiography.[20]
    Kirkwall Burgh School, formerly (and now again) known as the
Grammar School, was an important and historic institution.
Having been originally a Song School attached to St Magnus
Cathedral, and founded, according to tradition, by none other
than Bjarni Kolbeinson of Wyre, it could reasonably claim to be
among the oldest schools in Britain.[21] In the nineteenth century it
was one of 26 schools in Scotland called "burgh schools" and
administered by town councils: it was one of the smallest, and by
far the most northerly, of these schools.[22] The school provided
education for the children of Kirkwall regardless of social status
or academic ability. An interesting insight is given into the
inability of London and Edinburgh civil servants to understand
social conditions in Orkney by the initial refusal of the Scottish
Education Department to give grant to the school on the grounds
that it was " 'simply idle' to say that a school in which
mathematics and advanced Latin, Greek and French was taught
could be called a school for the working classes, and eligible for
grants under the Code." Only when the Inspector of Schools
submitted a list of pupils and their parents, showing that a large
proportion were the children of working men, did the Department relent.[23]

The educational opportunities open to Muir were certainly greater than those that would have been available to a boy from his social background almost anywhere else in Britain at that time; and, although he left the school when he was fourteen, Tom Scott's notion that "his conventional education consisted mainly of desultory attendance at a primary school" and that "even Burns was well-schooled by comparison"[24] is very wide of the mark.

His frequent absences, of course, militated against achievement. It was only when his family moved from the farm into Kirkwall that Muir enjoyed, in his own words, "one good year at school".[25] His memory of having to go home at one o'clock in the dead winter so as to get home before dark is almost certainly an exaggeration. Stanley Cursiter remembered being envious of Muir when the latter was released from school half an hour early to get home before dark.[26]

Several schoolmates of Muir have recorded their memories of him, though, since hindsight is not the most reliable guide, these memories have to be treated with some caution. The picture that they draw of his personality is, however, a consistent one. In 1959 Ernest Marwick wrote down the gist of a conversation he had had with James Groundwater who had been in the same class as Muir at Kirkwall Burgh School:

> He remembers Edwin as a very quiet boy, white-faced with little freckles around his nose. He was never, as far as Mr Groundwater remembers, top of his class, nor did he show any sign of special talent, but Mr Groundwater remembers even now what he calls "his pure, clear eye". "He was amazingly pure," he says. "I do not know if that means anything, but it is the only way I can describe it."[27]

Stanley Cursiter had a similar recollection of Muir's appearance and character but a rather higher opinion of his academic attainment:

> I first remember Edwin Muir when he came to Kirkwall School, a fair-haired, pale boy, in a light coloured suit with a Norfolk jacket neatly buttoned and the belt fastened.
> This impression of his being snugly buttoned up in a shy self-protection continued, but we in his class quickly found

that this seemingly colourless boy knew all the answers.
When examination times came he was always top—or near the
top—and we knew that Edwin was "different".[28]

In a radio interview given a few years after writing the above
Cursiter recalled that at school Muir "was not brilliant" but shone
at general knowledge.[29] Marion MacNeill, whose sister was in
Muir's class, remembered him well:

> Even as a boy of twelve, in his brown jersey and corduroy
> breeches he always had a groomed look that testified to a
> natural fastidiousness. He made a deep impression on one of
> my sisters, who shared his classes. It was not only his natural
> intelligence that struck her, but also a fineness of grain, and
> there was something in his pale serious face with its wide-set,
> far-seeing eyes that set him apart from the other boys.[30]

These reminiscences share the impression that Muir was "set
apart", was "different".

The level of his academic ability is less easy to assess. Unlike
Stanley Cursiter, Muir was not among the prize winners in 1901.
Nor did he gain a place in the bursary competition of 1900 when
several of his classmates, including Marion MacNeill's sister,
Florence, were successful. But along with Florence MacNeill and
others he was awarded a merit certificate.[31]

The teacher Muir remembered best was his English teacher,
Miss Annand, though he does not remember the spelling of her
name for in his autobiography he consistently refers to her as
"Miss Annan". He recalled her as "a remarkable woman" with
"endless charm, vitality, and patience."[32] He kept her photograph
for the rest of his life. Willa Muir sent it to Ernest Marwick after
her husband's death. On the reverse is written, in Willa Muir's
hand, "Edwin's beloved teacher at school, the one he learned most
from."[33] The photograph shows a young woman of undoubted
vitality; but her other qualities one must take on trust. The
impression that Miss Annand made on the poet is all the more
remarkable for the fact that she was a teacher in the Burgh School
for little more than four years—from January 1899 to February
1903.[34]

Kirkwall was undoubtedly a good school by the standards of its
time. The Inspectors' reports during the whole period that Muir

was a pupil there were consistently good, Miss Annand in particular being favourably mentioned. Muir's writing skills must have owed something to Miss Annand's teaching, just as it is likely they owed something to the work of Miss Angus. But it is questionable whether his schooling did much to stimulate the imagination of the future poet. This is not to say that the schooling offered at Kirkwall was entirely utilitarian. Scottish schools of the time had a less restricted curriculum than state schools in England, which, under the Code of 1870, were effectively bound to the teaching of reading, writing and arithmetic. In Scotland the value of music, for example, was widely acknowledged. The advertisement for a new teacher in Wyre in 1875 singled out music as "a recommendation". In 1899 an Inspector reported that in Kirkwall Burgh School, "singing is sweet and tuneful". And (not withstanding the views of General Burroughs) there was strong public support for the teaching of drawing.[35]

But the culture of Orkney's past, which had so much to offer the poet, was held in low esteem, as it was throughout the Highlands:

> The oral lore of the Highland people is rapidly dying out with the old people themselves. There is an essential difference between the old and young people. The young people are acquiring a smattering of school education in which they are taught to ignore the oral literature which tended to elevate and ennoble their fathers.[36]

An Orkney contemporary of Muir, John Mackay, wrote in 1960:

> I left school with the ability to read and write, and with certain fallacies deeply implanted in my mind. The most glaring of these fallacies were (1) that people who lived in Orkney were most unfortunate as they had no past history, (2) that the Orkney dialect was a kind of systematised bad English, and (3) the chief aim of education was to teach children to solve entirely useless examples in arithmetic.[37]

When not frowned on, the dialect was regarded with amusement. Henrietta Groundwater, having been given forty lines by her teacher for talking in class, copied the lines from a dialect poem by Walter Traill Dennison; her choice of poetry "greatly amused" both the teacher and Dr McEwen.[38]

Muir complained that the traditional syntax of Orkney speech, marked by a tendency to inversions, disappeared under the impact of education, and that local poets began to write "in an English laboriously learned from the grammar books."[39] The strength of the Burgh school lay in classics, mathematics and science. John W. Bews, who was three years ahead of Muir at school, and who became Principal of Natal University, was pleasantly surprised at a conference in Toronto to meet five fellow professors who had been at school with him in Orkney. They were all six scientists.[40] Most Orcadians are proud of the number of professors to have been educated in the islands. Not so Muir:

> The islands produce a terrible number of professors. But simple, uneducated people here and there still speak a beautiful language and know where to set a word in a sentence.[41]

For Muir, language is more important than knowledge, or is the highest kind of knowledge, and it is learned, not from grammar books, but from the life of the people. Language, at its most successful, binds together the work of the intellect and that of the imagination.

In Muir's schooldays Orkney had almost lost its traditional language but not, he thought, entirely. Only language could provide the link with the past that was necessary to his poetic imagination. School did not help to maintain that link. School may have helped his sentence construction, but it rejected both the culture of his forebears and the language which transmitted that culture. Muir could cling to the culture, or what was left of it, only through the memories of Wyre. For the rest of his life he worked on those memories from within.

Chapter Ten

# EXILE

WHEN MILTON'S archangel tells Eve that she and Adam must
leave Paradise, Eve exclaims at having to leave her "native soil":

> How shall we breathe in other air
> Less pure, accustomed to immortal fruits?

It was a cry that Eve's remote descendant, Edwin Muir, was to
echo throughout his life. As Margaret Bottrall says of him, "His
own life-pattern strikingly repeated the expulsion from the Garden, the shocking transition from a simple to a corrupt world."[1]
Daniel Hoffman, using a word that is frequently applicable to
Muir's poetry, says that Muir's uprooting from the place of his
birth became a "paradigm" for him of the Fall of Man.[2] Other
commentators have made much the same kind of observation. In
doing so they are either stating the obvious (that all men as they
grow up must leave behind a time of innocence) or attaching
themselves to a distinctive characteristic of Muir's thought and
personality. There is, I think, strong justification for such an
attachment. It is not merely that Muir, like Wordsworth, had a
particularly enduring nostalgia for the innocence of childhood; he
had, in addition, some difficulty in adapting to life in the corrupt
world outside the Garden, a difficulty that we are not aware of in
the case of Wordsworth. Muir's dilemma, like Eve's, was how,
accustomed to immortal fruits, he could breathe in other air, less
pure:

> 'This is time',
> Thought Adam in his dream, and time was strange
> To one lately in Eden.
>
> *Adam's Dream*

"I believe in the Fall," Muir wrote to William Soutar.[3] So, of course, do many men. The realization of the Fall is, Muir recognized, "a realization of a universal event."[4] Muir's Calvinist forebears saw it as the cause of the guilt and the worthlessness of individual men. Muir sometimes sees it in these terms too; but in most of his work it is the aspect of exile that is important. Paradise is a condition, or a stage in one's life, but above all it is a *place*, and the Fall is exclusion from that place. "The Fall," writes Muir in "Yesterday's Mirror", "drove me out of my seven years' Eden." It is a stage in growing up that he is talking about, but it is a stage that was, for him, marked by a change of address.

Muir never did have a permanent home. Even in Orkney he lived in five different houses before his fifteenth birthday. Thereafter his journeys through western Europe are marked by the milestones that head the chapters of his autobiography—Glasgow, Fairport, London, Prague, Dresden and Hellerau, Italy and Austria, England and France, Scotland, Prague again, and Rome. It is tempting to identify his early years in Orkney as the stage of innocence and his later life, particularly those terrible adolescent years in Glasgow, as that of experience. But such identification is just a little too simple, and carries with it the danger of allegorical interpretations of Muir's poems. The truth is that Muir instinctively grasped what anthropologists and historians of religion have concluded—that the myth of the Fall is so universal that it must be accounted among the oldest traditions of the human race. And the very universality of the myth made it attractive to him as a pattern which could clarify his own experience.

Exile is, of course, an important element of the Genesis version of the myth, in which exile is one of the results of man's disobedience. The other results, mortality and the need to work, feature much less prominently in Muir's work; and, indeed, in comparison with exile, hardly count as burdens at all. For Muir, man's alienation from the eternal is symbolized by his rejection from the place where he has been happy. The symbol includes the idea of a change of status but predominantly it expresses a change of place. Muir takes this aspect of the traditional myth and identifies it, not only with his own exile from Wyre, but also with the contemporary Orkney tragedy of evictions and emigration and with the wider literature of exile—the literature of Abraham and Moses and of Odysseus and Eurydice.

The removal of the Muir family from Wyre was not an "eviction" in the strict sense: they simply failed to renew their lease. The event did, however, fit into a pattern of eviction that had existed in the Highlands of Scotland for over a hundred years and that extended itself to the islands of Rousay, Egilsay and Wyre during the lifetime of James Muir. The memory of these evictions was readily embraced by the myth of the Garden of Eden.

By the middle of the nineteenth century the myth nationally had already centred itself on the clearances from the Sutherland estates during the first two decades of the century. The grim facts were known to everyone in the Highlands. In 1819, so that large sheep farms could be established, over a thousand eviction notices were served on tenants in the district of Strathnaver; the estate factor, Patrick Sellar, set about enforcing them. The minister of the parish, Donald Sage, watched with his own eyes the brutal eviction of his entire congregation and the burning of their cottages.[5] The victims, being not entirely illiterate, were able to bring their plight before the conscience of the nation. One of them, Donald Macleod, a stonemason, was able to write in 1857:

> I have devoted all my spare time and means, for the last
> thirty-four years, expostulating, remonstrating with, and
> exposing the desolations of my country, and the extirpation of
> my race, from the land of my birth.[6]

The nation was not allowed to forget Strathnaver, nor the other areas in the Sutherland estates where evictions took place. But the nation, of course, only partially listened to its conscience; Macleod, like many of his neighbours, had eventually to emigrate to Canada. What he and writers like him achieved was permanent affirmation of faith in a disappearing way of life. As Muir did in a more literary way, they saw this disappearance, simply yet profoundly, in terms of eviction from the place of one's birth. They were conscious of the need to record the truth for posterity. Macleod's own account of the events in Strathnaver ends with an assertion of his own reliability as a witness in words that echo the lines in St John's Gospel, "This is the disciple which testifieth of these things, and wrote these things: and we know that his testimony is true":

These proceedings were carried out with the utmost rapidity
as well as the most reckless cruelty. The cries of the victims,
the confusion, the despair and horror painted on the faces of
the one party, and the exulting ferocity of the other, beggar all
description. ... Many deaths ensued from alarm, from fatigue,
and cold; the people being instantly deprived of shelter, and
left to the mercy of the elements. ... To these scenes I was an
eye-witness, and am ready to substantiate the truth of my
statements, not only by my own testimony, but by that of
many others who were present at the time.

The biblical echoes can hardly be accidental. The gospel that
Macleod proclaimed was that man was born in innocence and was
evicted from Paradise through no fault of his own. Such a gospel
turns upside down the traditional Christian view of original sin:
Adam becomes the victim, not of his own pride, but of injustice.
Muir is, in "Outside Eden", not far from this heretical and
resentful position. But Muir, the Calvinist turned Socialist turned
Christian, is generally ambivalent on this matter. One cannot
always be sure whether he sees man as culprit or as victim.

Orkney too had its clearances. Significantly these were almost
peculiar to Rousay, Egilsay and Wyre. In 1840 the proprietor,
George William Traill, wrote to his factor that his first object in
the management of Wyre was to reduce its population and make it
into one compact farm.[7] In the event his ambitions for the island
were never realized, and indeed they were never publicly expressed. Where Traill did take action to reduce the population
was in two districts of Rousay itself. In 1845, deciding that the
district of Quandale, a narrow strip of land between the hill and
the sea, was too windswept to be suitable for the kind of improved
farms he hoped to establish in Wyre through gradual amalgam-
ations, Traill evicted twenty families and turned the whole area
into sheep pasture, enclosing it by six miles of stone dyke. Ten
years later he amalgamated the crofts in the district of Westness
into one large farm, evicting nine families in the process.[8] Further
evictions occurred in the same districts until, in 1883, the crofters
were able to tell the Napier Commission that forty families had
been evicted from the area. The number of people who lost their
homes was not great by the standards of Sutherland. But within
such a small community the evictions were deeply felt and long

remembered. The saying that Traill had "blawn the reek frae forty lums" passed into folklore. What made it worse was that the fact of eviction never became simply a past event. Many of those evicted became squatters on the hill outside the dyke that Traill built; Traill's successor, General Burroughs, was thought to have designs on this land too. It was as if a vengeful God had continued to harry Adam even after he had driven him from the Garden. Events, small in the eyes of the world, continued to loom large in the understanding of a people who refused to leave their little island. They chose the insecurity of squatting or, like the Muir family, of short-term leases. Living on the edge of Eden was preferable to the search for a new Paradise:

> Guilt is next door to innocence.
> So here this people choose to live
> And never think to travel hence.
>
> *Outside Eden*

Their insecurity was real because they continued to live close to the place where they had been hurled "headlong over the wall" and because their memories were long:

> The simple have long memories.
> Memory makes simple all that is.

Not everyone remained as squatters. Most emigrated. It takes an effort of will today to appreciate the atmosphere of a community in which news of the departure of yet another family must have been a weekly occurrence. The population of Rousay, Egilsay and Wyre declined by over a third between 1881 and 1911.[9]

While emigration was at its height in the Highlands generally in the first two decades of the century (with a fresh wave in the 1850s), the biggest emigration figures from Orkney were recorded during the decades 1861-1871 and 1881-1891. For Muir, therefore, emigration was a feature of the present, not of the recent past. "Great decrease in population," cried an *Orkney Herald* headline in connection with the drop in Orkney's population (from 32,044 to 30,171) shown by the 1891 census. But these figures actually understate the true position, the real level of emigration being masked by an increasing birth rate. Barclay shows that the number of people who left Orkney in the years 1861-1901 was 14,675—and this from a population of no more than 30,000. Emigration on this scale could only eat into the soul of a community. Could exile be any other than a major theme in Muir's poetry?

Those who controlled the expression of "received" opinion were almost unanimous in their advocacy of emigration as a solution to the economic problems of the Highlands. George William Traill wrote to Robert Scarth in 1843:

> Are there any other Rousay Tenants likely to follow the Example of Costie in seeking a settlement on the other side of the Atlantic? It would be very desirable to encourage so laudable a spirit of Enterprise.[10]

Exactly fifty years later another Orkney landlord spoke of emigration as the unquestioned ambition of every young man:

> The small farms supply labourers and the large farms employment, and any young man can as a farm servant soon earn sufficient money to convey himself to any of the colonies.[11]

The Orkney Landowners Association, petitioning parliament in 1886 to have Orkney excluded from the Crofters Act, claimed that Orcadians were so used to sailing the seas that they had no reluctance to emigrate. The argument is unconvincing and the conclusion conflicts with the evidence.

On every side education was seen as the great inducement to emigration. Several witnesses at the Napier Commission hearings claimed that education would lead the younger generation to see that there were better places in the world than the area where they lived. Sometimes the effect of education was even less subtle. In 1905 the Canadian government agent in Glasgow offered to send free wall maps of Canada to any school in Orkney.[12] H.M. Inspectors' Reports of the time lay great stress on wall maps.

The members of the Napier Commission[13] made shrewd use of the evidence put to them. "It will be found in the evidence," they reported, "that while the upper and middle classes resident in the crowded districts generally refer to emigration as the true solution to the crofter question, the crofters themselves express aversion to it." The commissioners had listened to people like the Rev. James Davidson of Skye who observed that "the more reduced in circumstances among the crofters are more averse to emigration than any others. It is surprising the tenacity with which they cling to their native soil." And like the Rev. James Ross, also of Skye, who told them: "The people are very fond of their native land. I believe they would not exchange their native hills and glens for any other place on the face of the habitable globe if they could remain at home." Such statements share the spirit of Muir's autobiography and his poetry.

A story told in Robertson's *Extermination of the Scottish Peasantry* is significant. An old man, asked by a stranger where the people from the empty houses in his glen had gone, replied, "They are out of my sight, and I do not know where they have gone." One is reminded of the opening lines of "The West":

> We followed them into the west,
> And left them there, and said good-bye.

For many, exile was as final as death itself

Opinion in Orkney among the "educated" classes was not entirely in favour of emigration. While many of the ministers who contributed to the Statistical Account of 1842 unthinkingly saw over-population as the cause for poverty, Robert Scarth, writing about the parish of Cross and Burness in Sanday, actually put forward a plea for immigration *into* Orkney, and a leader in the *Orkney Herald* in 1863 said, "We urge that we want all our labour—that we are in no need of emigration from our islands."[14] Both Scarth and the writer of the leader recognized that the islands needed capital as well as labour. Capital, alas, was not forthcoming.

The cost of emigration was not high. An advertisement in the *Orkney Herald* in 1888 offered passages to Canada for three pounds and to Australia for seven. James Muir could have taken his whole family to Canada for a sum equivalent to the annual rent of his farm. Like a minority of others he chose not to do so, but headed instead for the nearest large city. The move encountered problems which, if less dramatic than those met by some settlers in Canada, were in some ways as difficult to solve.

Macdonald's study of the shifting population of Scotland in the nineteenth century comments on the number of contemporary references to movement from the Highlands to the industrial Lowlands and suggests that this reflects, not the numerical strength of these migrants, but the extent to which the inhabitants looked on them as aliens in their manners, speech and religion. The Muir family were less alien in Glasgow than they might have been had they come from the Catholic and Gaelic-speaking areas of the West, but their manners were alien and they felt alien. Muir's autobiography and his novel, *Poor Tom*, give life to the migration statistics. His poem, "The Border", asks

> What shall avail me
> When I reach the border?

and he is forced to conclude:

> All, all will fail me,
> Tongue, foot and hand.
> Strange I shall hale me
> To that strange land.

Sixty years before Muir's description of Glasgow as a kind of vision of hell ("The crumbling houses, the twisted faces, the obscene words casually heard in passing, the ancient, haunting stench of pollution and decay, the arrogant women, the mean men, the terrible children"[15], Alister Robertson accused the Marquis of Breadalbane of sending his dispossessed tenants into "the vortex of vice and dissipation".[16] Muir's interpretation of Glasgow arose from more than the experience of a single family. He spoke for a whole people. Of course, what he saw was no different from what anyone else living in an industrial city at that time would have seen. "After a while," he wrote, "like everyone who lives in an industrial town, I got used to these things." What gives his observations the strength of vision is the shock of moving from one culture to another. One can call that shock the Fall.

In Glasgow Muir was, his wife wrote, "a displaced person".[17] As he saw more of the world he was to learn that the displacement of people was not confined to the Muir family and their neighbours. Even in the late nineteenth century a feeling for their native land was not, for the crofters of the Highlands and islands, an attachment to an abstraction. For a townsman "the land" had become a metaphor for the nation gathered in one place. But when a crofter spoke of "the land" he had in mind the physical soil, turf and rock from which he drew his livelihood. It is important to bear this in mind when reading Muir. When, for example, he writes,

> This is your native land.
> By ancient inheritance
> Your lives are free, though a hand
> Strange to you set you here ...
>
> *The Original Place*

the poet is creating an image of man's life on earth, but he is starting from a position where the "native land" metaphor is freshly derived from physical reality; and some of the conviction of experience does cling to the metaphor. These four lines encompass the idea that man's freedom is bound up with the inherited right to live in a particular place. Among the Highlanders this thinking was systematized into a theory of the clan system, in which the land belonged to the whole clan and the chiefs existed only to organize its defence. In Orkney, where the clan system was unknown, popular sentiment attached itself to a (no doubt mistaken) interpretation of Odal law under which peasants had an absolute right to their land.

There is a considerable body of written evidence to suggest that people held these theories, not only with tenacity, but with a surprising degree of understanding. In the introduction to his *Gloomy Memories in the Highlands of Scotland* Donald Macleod states his conviction that history justifies inalienable rights:

> Five hundred years before the Christian era the celts took
> possession of Scotland, and down from that period they
> governed themselves under the Patriarchal system, until the
> last remnant of it was destroyed upon the unfortunate muir of
> Cullodon; they had their kings and chieftains, who were
> entrusted with their government, not by hereditary rights,
> but as they were found competent to discharge their duties.

> They obeyed and ardently loved and respected their kings
> and chieftains while they behaved themselves, but no further;
> never allowed them to interfere with the rights of the land any
> further than to parcel it out to their followers impartially, and
> the people parcelled out to them what they considered suffi-
> cient to keep them comfortable and respectable.

This statement has a historical certainty about it that reminds one
of some of the revolutionary constitutions of the eighteenth
century. It was clearly intended as a serious argument, and it does
not stand alone. A speaker at Portree in 1885 stated that "Highlanders had never forgotten that the land was their's and that
landlordism was a violent encroachment upon the divine rights of
the people."[18] "The landlords are only stewards," proclaimed a
Land Law Reform Association meeting in Caithness in 1894.[19]

The Napier Commissioners recognized that explicit or implicit
in much of the evidence given to them by the Highland crofters
was a belief in the sanctity of custom as against law. They
encountered similar ideas in Orkney:

> The people of the Islands entertain a notion that they have
> been abusively deprived of certain rights and privileges which
> were secured to them under the conventions by which their
> country was ceded to the Crown of Scotland, and that if the
> institutions of their Norse ancestors had been preserved, the
> claims of the people to the use of the common pasture would
> not have been lost sight of in the partition of the commonty, if
> such partition, indeed, had ever been allowed. It seems prob-
> able that these impressions are altogether visionary.[20]

But custom carried little weight against statute. Highland chiefs,
who had town houses and belonged to London clubs, did not
share their tenants' view of their function and their status; those
who bought estates in Orkney were similarly unimpressed by
sentimental theories about Odal law. The law as it stood saw land
as little different from any other kind of property. General
Burroughs' comment on the popular cry, "The land is the
people's", was that the next cry would be, "The whisky is the
people's; the bread, meat, clothing, newspapers, houses are the
people's."[21]

In Orkney the nineteenth century was the century of enclo-
sures. At the beginning of the century nearly half the total area of
the county was common land, which meant in law that it was
owned jointly by the adjoining proprietors. But that is not how
the common people saw it. For generations they had been able to
graze their animals on the common, to remove peat from it for
fuel and stones to build their houses. When they had to they built
their houses on the common itself. These customary rights,
essential to the way of life of the poor, were swept away during
the course of the century. It is little wonder that the people, in
Hunter's words, "took refuge in a profound sense of betrayal".[22]
Little wonder that the men of Sutherland responded to criticisms
of a falling-off in recruitment to the Highland regiments with the
statement: "We do not know what we are to come forward for. We
have no country to fight for, as our glens and straths are laid
bare."[23]

This feeling that the land is empty and that there is no cause
left worth struggling for is to be found in Muir's poem,
"Scotland's Winter". The great men of the past—Percy, Douglas,
Bruce—all lie dead, together with

> all the kings before
> This land was kingless,
> And all the singers before
> This land was songless,
> This land that with its dead and living waits the
> Judgment Day.

The living, cut off from their attachment to the place, and with it
from all awareness of their glorious past, have little to add to the
achievements of the past.

Theories about customary land tenure were, to some extent,
rationalizations of the traditional yearning for the Golden Age,
seen in literary form in Hesiod and Ovid, and held by traditional
communities the world over. Koppers (in *Primitive Man and His
World Picture*) argues that so universal an idea that man once
lived in peace and happiness must either have been inspired by
memories of just such an age or have developed from man's
reflective powers. Muir's peasant contemporaries, who would

have had no difficulty in accepting the former explanation, set the Golden Age very recently indeed. Robertson argued historical fact against those who derided the memory of a happy peasantry as a sentimental myth: "The former condition of the peasantry seems to have drawn forth an unwarranted sneer. In reply to numerous inquiries, the answers all concur in representing the peaceful dwellers by the lake-side as peculiarly social. They lived without guile, they assisted each other in every respect, and nothing but harmony and good feeling prevailed."[24]

Walter Traill Dennison saw the Golden Age of Orkney as a historical fact too, though he set it rather further into the past:

> Prior to its impignoration, Orkney had achieved a higher point of civilization, both as regards government and social life, than any other county in the three Kingdoms. The Orcadian peasantry were the landlords of Orkney, owing vassalage to none.[25]

The belief that the Golden Age existed during, or just before, one's boyhood puts a particular burden on a man. It was a burden that Muir carried. His account of life in Wyre bears remarkable similarities to the statement of Robertson quoted above. But Muir's understanding of the myth of the Fall made him aware that the Golden Age is receding all the time.

The idea of the Golden Age enters Muir's poems in two images—the hill and the wall.

The image of the hill can only have been taken directly from the experience of Muir's neighbours in Orkney. For them the hill represented the freedom they had enjoyed for generations on the land outside the dyke. The hill is the place of eternal happiness:

> A single mountain on whose side
> Life blooms for ever and is still.
>
> *The Mountains*

The place where he lay as a child was "the sunny hill" of the poem, "Childhood". Exile took him away from the hill:

> But he has never
> Stood again upon that hill.
>
> *The Hill*

Since exile is forced from within as well as from without, the poet of "Scotland 1941" angrily associates himself with those who have destroyed the nation:

> We with such courage and the bitter wit
> To fell the ancient oak of loyalty,
> And strip the peopled hill and the altar bare,
> And crush the poet with an iron text,
> How could we read our souls and learn to be?

Final destruction is signalled by

> a hill split open
> With scraps of houses clinging to its sides,
> Stones, planks and tiles and chips of glass and china
> Strewn on the slope as by a wrecking wave
> Among the grass and wild-flowers.

This vision of the end of the world relates easily to the eye-witness accounts that survive of the Sutherland clearances.

The second image of the Golden Age has a rather more complex effect. To Muir walls speak of the glories of the past; when they are broken (as often they are) they spell the destruction of what men have achieved; they also, like the six miles of stone dyke that Traill built around the land of the displaced tenants of Quandale, signify exclusion. In Muir's poetry references to walls, and especially to broken walls, are remarkably frequent:

> And there he saw Troy built like a burial ground
> With tumbled walls for tombs, the smooth sward
> wrinkled
> As Time's last wave had long since passed that way.
>
> *Troy*

> We saw our houses falling
> Wall after wall behind us.
>
> *The Refugees*

> The green cross growing in a wood
> Close by old Eden's crumbling wall,

> And God himself in full manhood
> Riding against the Fall.

*The Human Fold*

> And all within the enclosure now,
> Light leaf and smiling flower, was false,
> The great wall breached, the garden dead.

*The Window*

The images of the hill and the wall combine at the end of "A Trojan Slave" to produce just the kind of elegaic statement that reflects men's memories of the good days in Rousay:

> Yet through that rage shines Troy's untroubled hill,
> And many a tumbled wall and vanished tree
> Remains, as if in spite, a happy memory.

The complaint of the Trojan slaves was that, even as Troy was falling, their masters had refused to arm them. The great ones did not see that for the common people too

> Troy was our breath, our soul, and all our wit,
> Who did not own it but were owned by it.

The great ones of Scotland and of Orkney did not see it either, did not see that, regardless of laws and leases, those on the land felt that they belonged there. When James Muir met his landlord, the little general, the man who believed that the land could be owned like whisky or newspapers, wandering over Wyre with his gun, there could be nothing but mutual incomprehension. For all that the poem is ostensibly set in Troy, the emotion it contains belongs to Rousay.

The two images of the hill and the wall meet again, this time in a distinctively Rousay setting, in the opening lines of "Outside Eden". The setting would, in its physical sense, be recognized by any visitor to Rousay today, but its emotion comes directly from the experience of exile:

> A few lead in their harvest still
> By the ruined wall and broken gate.

> Far inland shines the radiant hill.
> Inviolable the empty gate,
> Impassable the gaping wall;
> And the mountain over all.

The poem does not convey simple nostalgia for the days before the clearance; on the contrary, the conjunction of the images points to the ambiguities inherent in the idea of the pre-clearance days being the Golden Age. The wall which Traill built around Quandale excluded the tenants from their former homes: yet it did so by confining them to the common land on the hill which, as the "radiant hill", appears to express nostalgia for the Golden Age. The "country of this clan" is "haunted by guilt and innocence" and it is the "impassable" wall that seems to divide guilt from innocence.

The wall is impassable because there is no going back to innocence from guilt. The guilty can remember the days of innocence; but, as Adam discovered, knowledge, once gained, cannot be unlearned.

The wall is an ambiguous image, signifying both the civilization of the Golden Age and the eviction of men from it. The truth is that the Golden Age which the peasants of the nineteenth century talked about was not the true Golden Age but, like Troy itself, only a re-creation of it—one of the many re-creations of it, all of them doomed to crumble.

It is possible to assimilate the experience of eviction and emigration to the myth of the Fall only by modifying the traditional theology of the myth. In the Calvinist view, man owes his fallen state to his own worthlessness, and has no hope of returning to Paradise through his own efforts. The view of many of the protestors against evictions in the nineteenth century was that man would attain Paradise if only his rulers would let him. Muir, heir to both Calvin and Rousseau, ultimately rejects both these simplifications. Man, he finds, is neither simply a culprit nor a victim, but both.

Muir's poetry searches for an understanding of the human condition through the exploration of the memory, both collective and individual. He sees the nostalgia for Paradise, not as an escape from the human condition, but as a way of understanding it. The contribution of the myth to this process is not simply to explain once and for all how things came to stand as they do. Rather it allows perpetual repetition of the original event—in the history of Scotland, in the eviction of the Muir family and their neighbours, in Muir's own exile from childhood and from Orkney. And it demonstrates why Paradise is forever receding from view.

## Chapter Eleven

# RETURN

I INDICATED in Chapter One how often, throughout his life, Muir played with the idea of returning to Orkney. The idea of return is, in his poetry, almost as important a theme as exile itself. The idea is associated with the traditional belief that Paradise has not only been but is to come. Interest in Paradise myths is not necessarily purely nostalgic. Polak argues that idealized images of the past, expressed mainly in symbolic-poetic form, represent not only nostalgia for beginnings but images of the future, Paradise and the Golden Age being in this way transplanted from pre-history to the final stage of man.[1] Frank and Fritzie Manuel show that Utopias, discovered ostensibly in the past, are often in reality being justified for the future.[2]

The Golden Age ideas current in Orkney in Muir's youth were idealized pictures of the past alone. But Christian thinking projects the Paradise of pre-history into the future, and this is particularly true among prophets of the millennium. We know that, as a boy, Muir was familiar with millennial ideas. The family followed with interest the prophecies of Dr Baxter in the *Christian Herald* each week. We have some difficulty in believing that such ideas were taken seriously only a century ago, but we know from Muir's autobiography that they were indeed taken seriously in his household;[3] and there is some evidence that in Orkney the end of the world was not a subject to be pushed far into the future even in the most respectable ecclesiastical circles. A preacher addressing the Synod of Orkney in 1846, reminded his listeners, the assembled clergy of the Church of Scotland in Orkney, that the Bible contains many signs of "the terrible visitation of vengeance which should overtake the earth at the consummation of all things" and suggested that "in our days the predictions of all the prophets are rapidly fulfilling." The Synod was sufficiently impressed by this sermon to have it printed.[4]

The consummation of all things is the theme of four of Muir's major poems: "The Horses", "The Last War", "The Day before

155

the Last Day", and "The Transfiguration". The vision of "The Horses" puts the world back to a stage early in its history when man was at one with nature; it is a secularized and limited version of Paradise. In "The Last War" the poet despairs that history has failed to remedy itself:

> Did not have time to call on pity
> For all that is sick, and heal and remake our city.

In this view history has progressed too far for a Utopia based on the past to offer a future vision. The only release from pain lies in a "dream of pure commingled being". "The Day Before the Last Day" is perhaps the most despairing of all Muir's poems. All history is destroyed and, with it, even memory itself. For Muir there could be no greater despair. "Where and by whom shall we be remembered?" cry the people. Destruction, of course, has come from within. The wrong choice has been made; as in "The Last War", it is too late to unmake it. This is a constant theme in Muir. Acts cannot be unmade, knowledge unlearned. The despair expressed by this poem would be absolute, but for the qualifications, "Let us essay a hypothetical picture" and "Imaginary picture of a stationary fear".

All three of these images of the future derive from an angry reading of the present. To find a positive image based on the Christian faith and owing more than a little to the traditional millennial dreams that found their way to Muir through the pages of the *Christian Herald* one must turn to "The Transfiguration". Here the idea of the Second Coming allows history to be undone and the Paradise that has been and the Paradise that is to come to be drawn together. In the moment of Transfiguration the Paradise of the past erupts into the living present:

> The source of all our seeing rinsed and cleansed
> Till earth and light and water entering there
> Gave back to us the clear unfallen world.

It was a momentary vision, designed to inspire the world, not to restore it to what it was:

If it had lasted but another moment
It might have held for ever! But the world
Rolled back into its place, and we are here,
And all that radiant kingdom lies forlorn.

So the poet experiences the disappointment that comes from even
the most heroic visions of the Golden Age. What rescues hope
from nostalgia is faith in the Second Coming of Christ. Some day,
"when time is ripe", Christ will come again and Paradise will be
renewed on earth. The cross will be dismantled and grow again
into a tree "in a green springing corner of young Eden",

And Judas damned take his long journey backward
From darkness into light and be a child
Beside his mother's knee, and the betrayal
Be quite undone and never more be done.

This is not only a powerful statement of Muir's faith as a
Christian; it is also the resolution of the dilemma of exile and
return that lies at the heart of his poetry.

The traditional idea of the perpetual repetition of mythic
events, of the Fall and the restoration of the Golden Age, is one
that gives comfort to men in this life; and it is, as we have seen, an
idea that held a strong attraction for Muir, allowing him to
experiment in a symbolic way with the same themes again and
again. But ultimately, because of his Christian faith, he saw the
Fall, the Incarnation, and the Second Coming as unique events of
overwhelming importance. The Second Coming would indeed
restore man to primal innocence, and the Incarnation is the
promise that this is so. Within this unique framework there is
room for a model of human history in which the Fall is perpetu-
ally re-enacted and in which good men struggle to restore
Paradise or, at least, the limited historical Paradise that is the
Golden Age. Within that model Muir saw no value in the kind of
Utopia which simply wanted to start again without the benefit of
worthwhile human experience; he strongly criticised the revolutionary attitude that demanded a clean slate.[5] The Second
Coming of Christ restores men to total innocence; lesser strivings
for redemption have to be satisfied with recovering the best from
the past.

Even his nostalgia for Orkney was tempered by the knowledge that, since his departure, it had, in many ways, changed for the better:

> I paid a visit to two farms that my father had worked one after another. In his time it had been a hard job to wring a living from them and pay the rent; now they are very pleasant, easily worked and profitable places.[6]

He develops, too, the idea of the terrible sadness at the heart of nostalgia—that, however strong one's longing for the past, one may not, in the end, even wish to recover it. In "The Return" he imagines himself an old man revisiting his youth, seeing the sights he has longed for, hearing the voices that have recalled him, yet discovering that

> ... all within
> Rises before me there, rises against me,
> A sweet and terrible labyrinth of longing,
> So that I turn aside and take the road
> That always, early or late, runs on before.

Can there really be a road back from exile? The Greeks returning from Troy

> ...found a childish scene
> Embosomed on the past.
>
> *The Return of the Greeks*

The bitter truth is, Muir discovered, that nostalgia contains "a sweet and terrible labyrinth of longing", and that there is no easy way out of that labyrinth. In "Dialogue" the poet, "returning from the other side of time", believes he has found his home at last,

> But now, looking again, I see wall, roof and door
> Are changed, and my house looks out on foreign ground.
> This is not the end of the world's road.

# REFERENCES

## Chapter One: Orkney

1   *An Autobiography* 62.
2   ibid 11.
3   ibid 18.
4   Spender 1940, 778.
5   Read 1940, 984.
6   Leavis 1940, 171.
7   Hall 1956, 8.
8   Holloway 1955, 309.
9   Holloway 1960, 557.
10  Butter 1962, 45.
11  Wiseman 1978, 18.
12  Holloway 1955, 308.
13  Transcript in Orkney Archives D31/31/3/2.
14  *Latitudes* 24.
15  Brown 1955, 56.
16  Willa Muir 1968, 114.
17  25 March 1937. This and the other letters to Ernest Marwick and
    Robert Rendall quoted here are in the Orkney Archives D31/31/6,4.
18  *Orkney Herald* 13 January 1959.

## Chapter Two: The Island

1   *Orcadian* 10 August 1895.
2   Fergusson 1883, 87.
3   "In Search of Edwin Muir" (BBC broadcast, recorded 23 December
    1963, broadcast 28 April 1964.)
4   19 November 1936 (*Selected Letters* 93-94).
5   *Orcadian* 15 September 1891.
6   ibid 18 February 1893.
7   Free Church Minister 1846, 30.
8   Weld 1860, 166-167.
9   *An Autobiography* 60.
10  ibid 63.

11   ibid 64-65.
12   Nicoll 1920, 166-168.
13   *An Autobiography* 68.
14   ibid 55.
15   28 May 1940 (*Selected Letters* 121).
16   *Scottish Journey* 6.
17   *The Marionette* 37.
18   *An Autobiography* 92.
19   Brown 1955, 57.
20   Deedes 1935, 3-42.
21   *An Autobiography* 67.
22   ibid 32.
23   *Essays on Literature and Society* 121.
24   Eliade (1949) 1955, 17-18.

## Chapter Three: Family

1   *An Autobiography* 11.
2   Orkney Archives D31/35/3c.
3   ibid.
4   *Orkney Herald* 9 March 1887.
5   *An Autobiography* 11.
6   17 October 1956 (*Selected Letters* 188-189).
7   *Scott and Scotland* 181.
8   Letter to George Thorburn, 14 May 1927 (*Selected Letters* 64).
9   *An Autobiography* 62.
10   Ployen (1840) 1894, 167.
11   Munch 1853 (*Orkney Herald* 25 August 1863).
12   Brown 1955, 55.
13   New Statistical Account 34-40, 107; Pringle 1874, 27.
14   *Daily Free Press* 18 May 1891.
15   Wilson 1928, 149.
16   *Orcadian* 23 January 1892.
17   Orkney Archives D19/1/1 and D19/2/5.
18   *An Autobiography* 58-59.
19   Willa Muir 1968, 137.
20   *An Autobiography* 24-25.
21   quoted in *Selected Letters* 210.
22   Interview, 24/9/71 (Orkney Archives D31/2/4).
23   *An Autobiography* 16.
24   ibid 16-18.
25   ibid 104.

26  Willa Muir 1965, 53-54.
27  *Poor Tom* 93.
28  *An Autobiography* 18.
29  Firth (1920) 1974, 78.
30  UP Church 1883, 5.
31  Orkney Church Records 21/3.
32  Orkney Archives D31/39/3.
33  see Maxwell 1966, 101.
34  *An Autobiography* 19-20.
35  ibid 20.
36  Firth (1920) 1974, 13.
37  Brown 1955, 54.
38  Marwick, *The Sufficient Place* 3-4.
39  *An Autobiography* 21.
40  ibid 66.
41  *Poor Tom* 242.

## Chapter Four: The Farm

1  Huberman 1971, 150.
2  Franklin 1969, 1-2.
3  ibid 44.
4  *An Autobiography* 63.
5  *The Estate of Poetry* 1.
6  March 1939, quoted in Butter 1966, 163.
7  *Scottish Journey* 71.
8  Eliade (1957) 1960, 164.
9  eg Maringer (1956) 1960, 134.
10  Eliade (1957) 1960, 37.
11  *The Story and the Fable* 263.
12  Orkney Archives D31/1.
13  ibid D31/3/2; *Orcadian* 9 October 1969.
14  *An Autobiography* 48.
15  ibid 36.
16  Butter 1962, 50-51; Huberman 1971, 41.
17  *An Autobiography* 22.
18  *Poor Tom* 172-174.
19  Maringer (1956) 1960, 187; Davidson 1967, 90; Turville-Petrie 1964, 251.
20  Solheim 1956, 160-173.
21  Old Statistical Account xvi-xvii.
22  ibid 234.

23   Solheim 1956, 109.
24   Low 1773, 50; Barry 1805, 324-325; Firth (1920) 1974, 118.
25   *An Autobiography* 13-14.
26   see Henderson 1967.
27   Orkney Archives D31/2/1.
28   Evans 1966, 235; Macpherson 1929, 290-291; Carter 1979, 144-147.


Chapter Five: The Fable

1    *An Autobiography* 63.
2    ibid 29; *Orcadian* 5 October 1961; Willa Muir 1965, 105.
3    Child 1882-1898, vol II, 20.
4    *An Autobiography* 28-30, 41.
5    Dennison 1880, xiii.
6    Firth (1920) 1974, 20.
7    ibid 38.
8    Dennison (1891) 1961, 25.
9    Hall 1956, 9.
10   Orkney Archives D31/4/1.
11   Briggs 1967, 3.
12   Marwick's notebooks are in the Orkney Archives.
13   Dennison (1891) 1961, 63-64.
14   ibid 44.
15   *An Autobiography* 14.
16   Orkney Archives D31/1/6.
17   Marwick 1949. 15.
18   *Orcadian* 29 August 1968.
19   Brown 1955, 55.
20   *Scottish Journey* 46.
21   Dennison 1893, 173.
22   *An Autobiography* 62.
23   Barry 1805, 222; Dennison 1880, x-xi; Geipel 1971, 105-106.
24   Hoffman 1967, xiii, 233-236.
25   Dennison (1891) 1961, 2-3.
26   Willa Muir 1968, 45.
27   *An Autobiography* 28, 57.
28   ibid 28.
29   ibid 73.
30   ibid 75-76.
31   ibid 13.
32   Orkney Archives D31/1/4 and D31/2/6.
33   *An Autobiography* 77.

34  Child 19; Collinson 258.
35  Willa Muir 1965, 97-98.
36  Dennison (1891) 1961, 1-2.
37  *An Autobiography* 78-79.
38  *Orcadian* 15 March 1856.
39  Goodfellow 1912, 374-375.
40  Wiseman 1978, 191.
41  Eliade (1957) 1960, 32-33.

## Chapter Six: The Estate

1   *The Estate of Poetry* 9.
2   *The Story and the Fable* 263.
3   Hall 1956, 18.
4   Wiseman 1978, 18.
5   Butter 1962, 2.
6   The estate accounts of Rousay and Wyre, together with the private
    papers of General Burroughs, are held in the Orkney Archives.
    Extensive reference to them is made in this chapter. A further source
    of information on the estate is in the printed evidence of the Napier
    Commission.
7   Pringle 1874, 63. For the state of agriculture in Orkney see also
    Laing (1837) 1856, and Ployen (1880) 1894.
8   Note book of Mr Marwick of Corse (Orkney Archives D8/1/22).
9   These events are described in some detail in Hunter's *The Making of
    the Crofting Community*, 1976.
10  See Napier Report and printed evidence of the Napier Commission.
    Burroughs' own collection of press cuttings on his dispute with his
    tenants, drawn from 16 periodicals and covering 200 pages of double
    columns, is preserved in the Orkney Archives.
11  *The Orcadian* and the *Orkney Herald* carried full accounts of the
    hearings of the Crofters Commission in August and September
    1888. For Burroughs' subsequent disputes with his tenants see his
    correspondence with his solicitors (Orkney Archives D19/6) and the
    Report of the Deer Forests Commission 1895.
12  Raine 1967, 6.
13  *Orkney Herald* 22 August 1883.
14  Deer Forests Commission, 1127 and 1150.
15  *An Autobiography* 66.
16  6 December 1954 (quoted in Butter 1966, 3).
17  Information about the weather can be found in Spence 1908, Moar
    1931, and in the newspapers of the time.

18  *An Autobiography* 39-40.
19  Huberman 1971, 38.
20  *The Estate of Poetry* 9; letter to Stephen Spender, 19 June 1936 (*Selected Letters* 93).
21  *An Autobiography* 59.
22  Huberman 1971, 118.
23  Brown 1966 (*Orcadian* 15 December 1966).

## Chapter Seven: The Tribe

1  Ramsay 1873, 5.
2  *An Autobiography* 33.
3  Free Church Minister 1846, 30; Pringle 1874, 6; Fergusson 1883, 156; Kerr 1902, 173.
4  *An Autobiography* 25-26; Orkney Archives D31/30/4; Dennison 1880, xvi.
5  *An Autobiography* 44-45.
6  ibid 63.
7  Linklater 1938, 8.
8  *Scottish Journey* 111; Willa Muir 1968, 23; *An Autobiography* 93; *Scottish Journey* 112.
9  Orkney Archives D31/7/1.
10  Rabelais 301.
11  Orkney Archives D31/1/1 and D31/1/6.
12  *An Autobiography* 56.
13  "Yesterday's Mirror" 404.
14  Willa Muir 1968, 176.
15  24 August 1949 (*Selected Letters* 153).
16  *Scottish Journey* 238.
17  Willa Muir 1968, 256, 304, 292.
18  *Social Credit* 12.
19  Neill 1806.
20  Thomson 1981, 86.
21  *Postal Communications* 4; *Orkney Herald* 6 July 1885.
22  *Orkney Herald* 6 December 1876, 23 April 1877, 26 September 1888; *Orcadian* 21 December 1878, 12 April 1879.
23  *Orkney Herald* 4 June 1870.
24  ibid 2 August 1870.
25  ibid 12 April 1905.
26  19 February 1884 (Orkney Archives D19/8/12/2).
27  *Daily Free Press* 18 May 1891.
28  Letter to Mrs Inkster, 9 October 1901 (Orkney Archives D19).

29  Orkney Archives D19/6 and D19/2/2.

30  Hunter 1976, 91.

31  *Orkney and Zetland Telegraph* 25 March 1880.

32  *Orkney Herald* 5 September 1883.

33  E.W.Marwick to Robert Rendall, 4 May 1956 (Orkney Archives D31/34/1).

34  John Gibson to Burroughs, 24 November 1892 (Orkney Archives D19/8/13).

35  *Orkney Herald* 14 December 1892.

36  Firth (1920) 1974, 32.

37  Orkney Archives D31/7/1.

38  *Orkney Herald* 24 August 1894; *Orcadian* 15 September 1894; Memorial 1893; Orkney Archives D19/17/13 and D19/7/10.

39  *Scotsman* 28 March 1894; *Orcadian* 3 October 1896.

40  10 September 1958 (*Selected Letters* 207).

## Chapter Eight: The Church

1   *Orkney Herald* 20 December 1980.

2   *An Autobiography* 277.

3   *Selected Letters* 107.

4   ibid 115.

5   BBC Broadcast 28 April 1964; Willa Muir to Ernest Marwick, 17 November 1966 (Orkney Archives D31/31/6); Ernest Marwick to Mlle Dodat, 3 March 1966 (Orkney Archives D31).

6   The Session Records of the Church of Scotland, the United Presbyterian Church and the Free Church congregations of Holm, Rousay and Kirkwall are all housed in St Magnus Cathedral, Kirkwall.

7   *An Autobiography* 27.

8   Hossack 1900, 459.

9   For a general history of religion in Scotland in the nineteenth century see the two volumes of Drummond and Bulloch, 1975 and 1978; for the origins of the Secession Church see Thomson 1848; for contemporary accounts of belief and practice in the United Presbyterian Church see Mackelvie 1873 and Blair 1888.

10  Webster 1910, 1.

11  Mackelvie 1873, 551-557.

12  *British Weekly* 18 October 1894.

13  Thomson 1848, 65.

14  Buchan 1835, 31.

15  Leckie 1926, 218.

16   George William Traill to Robert Scarth, 30 May 1844 (private collection).
17   *Glasgow Herald* 22 January 1850; Orkney Archives D31/35/39.
18   Scarth to Burroughs, 27 February 1874 (Orkney Archives D19/8/11).
19   Quoted in Webster 1910, 108,109.
20   *Orkney Herald* 24 September 1884.
21   Information on the School Board is taken from the minutes of the Board (Orkney Archives CO5/17/1 and from reports in the *Orkney Herald*, the *Orcadian*, *Christian Leader* and the *Scotman*.
22   Assignation and receipts (Orkney Archives D19/6/8); F. Borthwick to Burroughs, 14 July 1889 (Orkney Archives D19/8/13).
23   *An Autobiography* 231.
24   *John Knox* 99.
25   Muir to Sydney Schiff, 8 July 1929 (*Selected Letters* 66).
26   26 January 1940 (*Selected Letters* 114).
27   *John Knox* 116.
28   *An Autobiography* 107.
29   *The Three Brothers* 201.
30   *John Knox* 224.
31   *Scottish Journey* 36.
32   *John Knox* 306-307.
33   Campbell (1856) 1959, 79; Campbell 1831, xxiv.
34   United Presbyterian 1858, 9.
35   Webster 1910, 73.
36   George William Traill to Scarth, 29 January 1844 (private collection).
37   Macleod 1841, xv.
38   Thomson 1981, 52.
39   *Orkney Herald* 24 September 1884.
40   *Orcadian* 11 December 1886.
41   Vincent (1966) 1972, 86.
42   Neil Rose to George Learmonth, 10 December 1868 (Orkney Archives D19/8/10).
43   *Edinburgh Courant* 16 December 1868.
44   *John Knox* 113.
45   Webster 1910, 103.
46   *An Autobiography* 84 and 85-88.
47   Eliade 1959, 163-164; Davidson 1967, 15.
48   Barry 1805, 342.
49   Old Statistical Account 341; Clouston 1862, 21; McPherson 1929, 3, 14-15, 112; Firth (1920) 1974, 76; Dennison 1880, 85.
50   *Orkney Herald* 21 May 1957.

51  Orkney Archives D31/2/2.
52  Marwick 1975, 95.
53  *An Autobiography* 280.
54  ibid 277.
55  ibid 247.
56  *Social Credit* 11.
57  Fergusson 1883, 25-26.
58  Ployen (1840) 1894, 148.
59  Church in Orkney 1844, 7.
60  Marwick, *The Sufficient Place*.
61  Muir to Ernest Marwick, 13 April 1955 (Orkney Archives D31/31/6).
62  *An Autobiography* 278.
63  *The Three Brothers* 317.

## Chapter Nine: School

1   *Orcadian* 21 September 1901.
2   *An Autobiography* 41.
3   24 January 1961 (Orkney Archives D31/31/6).
4   *An Autobiography* 70.
5   Ramsay 1873, 2, 4, 5.
6   The Minutes of the Board are in the Orkney Archives CO5/17/1.
7   Napier Report 77; Ramsay 1873, 6.
8   *Orkney Herald* 4 November 1896.
9   *An Autobiography* 40, 71.
10  Orkney Collection, Orkney Library.
11  *Orcadian* 12 November 1881.
12  ibid 12 October 1901.
13  *Orkney Herald* 18 August 1875; later reports on Wyre School by H.M.Inspectors were published in the *Orkney Herald* on 27 September 1876, 13 August 1884, 23 September 1885, and 19 September 1894.
14  *An Autobiography* 41; ibid 40-42.
15  ibid 41.
16  *The Three Brothers* 38.
17  *An Autobiography* 42.
18  "Childhood" (*Collected Poems* 19).
19  Admissions Register of Kirkwall Burgh School 1878-1896 (Orkney Archives CO5/80/10). Muir was number 1613.
20  *An Autobiography* 68-69.
21  Mooney 1947, 137; Fereday 1976, 7.
22  Grant 1876, 440-441.

23  Kerr 1902, 75.
24  Scott 1977/1978, 29.
25  *An Autobiography* 71.
26  Cursiter 1976, 34.
27  Recorded in a letter to Dr A.C.Hixsen, 24 April 1971 (Orkney Archives D31/31/6).
28  Cursiter 1959.
29  BBC broadcast 23 December 1963.
30  MacNeill, "Memories of Edwin Muir".
31  Minute of the County Committee on Secondary Education, 21 July 1900 (Orkney Archives CO5/3/2); Kirkwall Burgh School Log Book (Orkney Archives CO5/8/1).
32  *An Autobiography* 71.
33  Orkney Archives D31/31/4.
34  Minutes of the Combined School Board of Kirkwall and St Ola, 23 November 1898 (Orkney Archives CO5/13/4); Kirkwall Burgh School Log Book, 20 February 1903 (Orkney Archives CO5/8/1).
35  Kirkwall Burgh School Log Book (Orkney Archives CO5/8/1); *Orcadian* 17 August 1901.
36  Statement by Alexander Carmichael, Napier Report 473.
37  Mackay 1960.
38  MS Memories (Orkney Archives D31/38/2).
39  *An Autobiography* 62.
40  Bayer 1976, 25.
41  *An Autobiograpy* 63.

## Chapter Ten: Exile

1  Bottrall 1960, 180.
2  Hoffman 1967, 226.
3  3 February 1940 (*Selected Letters* 115-117).
4  *An Autobiography* 114.
5  Sage 1889, 216.
6  Macleod (1841, 1857) 1892.
7  George William Traill to Robert Scarth, 19 December 1840 (MS in private collection).
8  For information on the evictions in Rousay see Thomson 1981, 47-52; Napier Evidence 1535; Marwick, *Journey from Serfdom*; Orkney Sound Archives 18.
9  For population figures see Moira and Moira 1960, part 1, 187; Barclay 1951; *Orkney Herald* 29 April 1891.
10  MS in private collection.

11  Paper read by Johnston of Coubister to the Viking Club of London (*Orkney Herald* 24 May 1893).
12  *Orkney Herald* 31 August 1904.
13  Napier Report 101-102 and Appendices 8, 59, 117.
14  *Orkney Herald* 24 February 1863.
15  *An Autobiography* 91-92.
16  Robertson 1853, 6.
17  Willa Muir 1968, 18.
18  *Oban Times* 5 September 1885.
19  *Northern Ensign* 20 February 1894.
20  Napier Report 28-29; see also page 8 of the Report.
21  *People's Journal* 4 March 1883.
22  Hunter 1976, 14.
23  Ross 1856, 4.
24  Robertson 1853, 19.
25  Dennison 1880, xvi.

## Chapter Eleven: Return

1  Polak 1961, 26, 30-31.
2  Manuel 1979, 5.
3  *An Autobiography* 28.
4  Brotchie 1846.
5  *Social Credit and the Labour Party*.
6  *Scottish Journey* 240.

# LIST OF SOURCES

## 1. MANUSCRIPT SOURCES

ORKNEY ARCHIVES, Orkney Library, Laing Street, Kirkwall, Orkney.
CHURCH RECORDS, St Magnus Cathedral, Kirkwall, Orkney.
PRIVATE COLLECTION of letters by G.W. Traill and R. Scarth.

## 2. WORKS BY EDWIN MUIR
This list contains only those works to which reference is made in the text. The place of publication is in every case London.

*An Autobiography* 1954 (reissued 1980).
*Collected Poems 1921-1958* (1960), revised edition 1965.
*Essays on Literature and Society* (1949), revised edition 1965.
*The Estate of Poetry* 1962.
*John Knox: Portrait of a Calvinist* 1929.
*Latitudes* 1924.
*The Marionette* 1927.
*Poor Tom* 1932.
*Scottish Journey* 1935.
*Selected Letters of Edwin Muir*, edited by P.H.Butter, 1974.
*Social Credit and the Labour Party* 1935.
*The Story and the Fable* 1940.
*The Three Brothers* 1929.
"Yesterday's Mirror, Afterthoughts of an Autobiography" (*Scots Magazine* September 1940, pp 405-410).

## 3. OTHER BOOKS AND ARTICLES
Again, this list contains only those works to which reference is made in the text. Except where stated otherwise, the place of publication is London.

BALFOUR, D.: *Ancient Orkney Melodies*, Edinburgh 1885.
BARCLAY, R.S.: "Volume of Emigration Since 1861" (*Orcadian* Nov. 1951).
BARRY, G.: *The History of the Orkney Islands*, Edinburgh 1805.

170

BAYER, A.W.: "John Bews: One of the Burgh School's Professors" (*Kirkwall Grammar School*, edited by W.P.L.Thomson, Kirkwall, 1976).

BLAIR, W.: *The United Presbyterian Church, A Handbook of its History and Principles*, Edinburgh 1888.

BOTTRAL, M.: Review of Muir's *Collected Poems* (*Critical Quarterly* II, Summer 1960, 179-180).

BRIGGS, K.: *The Fairies in Tradition and Literature*, 1967.

BROTCHIE, J.: *The Church and the Dissenters*, Edinburgh 1834.

BROWN, G.M.: "Living in Orkney" (*Saltire Review* vol.2, no.6, Winter 1955, 54-60).

BUCHAN, P.: *Remarks on the Rev Ebenezer's Defence of Civil Establishments of Religion*, Edinburgh 1835.

BUTTER, P.H.: *Edwin Muir*, Edinburgh 1962.

BUTTER, P.H.: *Edwin Muir, Man and Poet*, Edinburgh 1966.

CAMPBELL, J.M.: Anon.: *Whole Proceedings in the Case of the Rev. John Macleod Campbell*, Greenock 1831.

CAMPBELL, J.M.: *The Nature of the Atonement* (1856) 1959.

CARTER, I.: *Farmlife in Northeast Scotland 1840-1914*, Edinburgh 1979.

CHILD, F.J.: *The English and Scottish Popular Ballads* (10 parts, 1882-1898), 5 volumes, New York 1965.

CHURCH IN ORKNEY: Anon: *The Church in Orkney, Address to Members of the Established Church on the Secession*, Edinburgh 1844.

CLOUSTON, C.: *Guide to the Orkney Islands*, Edinburgh 1862.

CLOUSTON, J.S.: *Records of the Earldom of Orkney 1299-1614*, Edinburgh 1914.

COLLIER, A.: *The Crofting Problem*, Cambridge 1953.

COLLINSON, F.: *The Traditional and National Music of Scotland* (1966) 1978.

COMMITTEE ON MORALS: *Report of the Committee on Morals appointed by the Synod of Orkney*, Kirkwall 1884.

CURSITER, S.: (Edwin Muir) "An Appreciation" (*Orcadian* 8 Jan. 1959).

CURSITER, S.: Clark and Sclater, "An Interview with Dr Stanley Cursiter" (*Kirkwall Grammar School*, edited by W.P.L.Thompson, Kirkwall 1976, pp 33-34).

DAVIDSON, H.R.E.: *Pagan Scandinavia*, 1967.

DEEDES, C.M.: "The Labyrinth" (*Myth and Ritual*, edited by S.H.Hooke, Oxford 1933, pp 3-42).

DEER FORESTS COMMISSION: *Minutes of Evidence Taken before the Royal Commission (Highlands and Islands 1892)*, Edinburgh 1895.

DENNISON, W.T.: *The Orcadian Sketch-Book*, Kirkwall 1880.

DENNISON, W.T.: *Orkney Folklore and Traditions* (1891), edited by E.W. Marwick, Kirkwall 1961.

DENNISON, W.T.: Notes on Orkney Folklore (*Scottish Antiquary* vol. VIII, 1893.)

DRUMMOND, A.L. & BULLOCH, J.: *The Church in Victorian Scotland 1843–1874*, Edinburgh 1975.

DRUMMOND, A.L. & BULLOCH, J.: *The Church in Late Victorian Scotland 1874-1900*, Edinburgh 1978.

ELIADE, M.: *The Myth of the Eternal Return* (1949), translated by W.R.Trask, 1955.

ELIADE, M.: *Myths, Dreams and Memories* (1957), translated by P.Mairet, 1960.

ELIADE, M.: *The Sacred and the Profane* (1957), translated by W.R.Trask, New York 1959.

EVANS, G.E.: *The Pattern Under the Plough*, 1966.

FEREDAY, R.P.: "Sang School to Burgh School" (*Kirkwall Grammar School*, edited by W.P.L.Thomson, 1976, pp 7-28.)

FERGUSSON, R.M.: *Rambles in the Far North* (1883) 2nd edition, Paisley 1884.

FIRTH, J.: *Reminiscences of an Orkney Parish* (1920), Stromness 1974.

FRANKLIN, S.H.: *The European Peasantry, the Final Phase*, 1969.

FRAZER, J.: *The Golden Bough*, abridged edition 1922.

"FREE CHURCH MINISTER": *Notes on a Tour in Orkney and Shetland, September 1845*, Inverness 1846.

GEIPEL, J.: *The Viking Legacy*, Newton Abbot 1971.

GOODFELLOW, A.: *Sanday Church History*, Kirkwall 1912.

GORRIE, D.: *Summers and Winters in the Orkneys* (1868), 2nd ed. 1869.

GRANT, J.: *History of the Burgh Schools in Scotland*, 1876.

GREIG, G.: *Last Leaves of Traditional Ballads and Ballad Airs*, edited by A. Keith, Aberdeen 1925.

HALDANE, J.A. (with J.Aikman and J.Rate): *Journal of a Tour Through the Northern Counties of Scotland and the Orkney Isles in Autumn 1797*, Edinburgh 1798.

HALL, J.C.: *Edwin Muir*, 1956.

HEARN, S.G.: "Edwin Muir: the Man and His Work" (*Books in Scotland*, no.9, 1981, pp 6-7).

HENDERSON, H.: "The Horseman's Word" (*Scots Magazine*, May 1967).

HOFFMAN, D.: *Barbarous Knowledge, Myth in the Poetry of Yeats, Graves, and Muir*, New York 1967.

HOLLOWAY, J.: "Enacted on a Distant Isle" (*Hudson Review* VIII, Summer 1955, pp 308-313).

HOLLOWAY, J.: "The Poetry of Edwin Muir" (*Hudson Review* XIII, 1960, pp 550-567).

HOSSACK, B.H.: *Kirkwall in the Orkneys*, Kirkwall 1900.

HUBERMAN, E.: *The Poetry of Edwin Muir, The Field of Good and Evil*, New York 1971.

HUNTER, J.: *The Making of the Crofting Community*, Edinburgh 1976.

KERR, J.: *Memories Grave and Gay*, 1902.

KOPPERS, W.: *Primitive Man and his World Picture*, 1952.

LAING, S.: *Journal of a Residence in Norway During the Years 1834, 1835, and 1836*, (1837) 1856.

LEAVIS, Q.D.: "The Literary Life Respectable" (*Scrutiny* IX, September 1940, pp 170-173).

LECKIE, J.H.: *Secession Memories, The United Presbyterian Contribution to the Scottish Church*, Edinburgh 1926.

LINKLATER, E.: "The Orkney Farmers" (*Scotland 1938, Twenty-five Impressions*, edited by J.R.Allan, Edinburgh 1938.)

LOW, G. *A Tour Through the Islands of Orkney and Shetland* (written 1774), Inverness 1879.

MACKAY, J.D.: "Reflections on Education" (*New Shetlander*, Yule 1960).

MACKELVIE, W.: *Annals and Statistics of the United Presbyterian Church*, Edinburgh 1873.

MACLEOD, D.: *Gloomy Memories in the Highlands of Scotland* (1841,1857) Glasgow 1892.

McNEILL, F.M.: "Memories of Edwin Muir" (*Jabberwocky* vol. 6, n.d. pp 22-23).

McPHERSON, J.M.: *Primitive beliefs in the North-East of Scotland*, 1929.

MANUEL, F.E. & F.P.: *Utopian Thought in the Western World*, Oxford 1979.

MARINGER, J.: *The Gods of Prehistoric Man* (1956) 1960.

MARWICK, E.W.: (editor) *An Anthology of Orkney Verse*, Kirkwall 1949.

MARWICK, E.W.: *The Sufficient Place: Memories of an Island Childhood*, unpublished MS, n.d. (c. 1965), (Orkney Archives D31/25/1).

MARWICK, E.W.: *The Folklore of Orkney and Shetland*, 1975.

MOAR, W.J.: "Climate and Weather of Orkney" (*Journal of the Orkney Agricultural Discussion Society*, Kirkwall, vol. 6, 1931, pp 8-16).

MOIRA AND MOIRA: *County Survey of Orkney*, Kirkwall (Orkney County Council) 1960.

MOONEY, J.: *The Cathedral and Royal Burgh of Kirkwall* (1943), Kirkwall 1947.

MUIR, W.: *Living with Ballads*, 1965.

MUIR, W.: *Belonging, a Memoir*, 1968.

NAPIER EVIDENCE: *Evidence Taken by Her Majesty's Commissioners of Inquiry into the Condition of the Crofters and Crofting in the Highlands and Islands of Scotland*, Edinburgh 1884.

NAPIER REPORT: *Report of Her Majesty's Commissioners of Inquiry into the Condition of the Crofters and Cottars in the Highlands and Islands of Scotland*, Edinburgh 1884.

NEW STATISTICAL ACCOUNT: *The Statistical Account of the Orkney Islands*, Edinburgh 1842.

NICOLL, M.: *Dream Psychology*, 2nd. edition 1920.

OLD STATISTICAL ACCOUNT: *The Statistical Account of Scotland 1791-1799*, reissue, Wakefield 1978, vol. XIX, Orkney and Shetland.

*ORKNEYINGA SAGA*, tr. Palsson and Edwards, 1978.

PLOYEN, C.: *Reminiscences of a Voyage to Shetland, Orkney and Scotland* (Copenhagen 1840), tr. C.Spence, Lerwick 1894.

POLAK, F.L.: *The Image of the Future*, tr. E. Boulding, Leyden 1961.

POSTAL COMMUNICATIONS: *The Postal Communication with the Orkney Islands*, Kirkwall n.d. (1853?).

PRINGLE, R.O.: "On the Agriculture of the Islands of Orkney" (*Transactions of the Highland and Agricultural society of Scotland*, 4th series, vol. VI, 1874).

RABELAIS: *Gargantua and Pantagruel*, tr. J.M. Cohen, 1955.

RAINE, K.: *Defending Ancient Springs*, 1967.

RAMSAY, G.M.: *Report to the Board of Education for Scotland on the Local Educational Circumstances of Orkney and Shetland*, Edinburgh 1873.

READ, H. "Life Relived" (*Listener* XXIII, 16 May 1940, 984).

ROBERTSON, A. ("R.Alister"): *Extermination of the Scottish Peasantry*, Edinburgh 1853.

ROSS, D.: *Letters on the Depopulation of the Highlands*, Edinburgh 1856.

SAGE, D.: *Memorabilia Domestica*, Wick 1889.

SCOTT, T.: "Orkney's Greatest Poet, Edwin Muir" (*Scotia Review* 18, 1977/1978, pp 29-37).

SOLHEIM, S.: *Horse-fight and Horse-race in Norse Tradition*, Oslo 1956.

SPENCE, M.: "The Climate of Orkney" (*Journal of the Scottish Meteorological Society*, vol. XIV, n. XXV, 1908).

SPENDER, S.: "Being Alive", review of *The Story and the Fable* (*New Statesman*, 22 June 1940, pp 777-778).

THOMSON, A.: *Historical Sketch of the Origin of the Secession Church*, Edinburgh 1848.

THOMSON, W.P.L.: *The Little General and the Rousay Crofters*, Edinburgh 1981.

TURVILLE-PETRE, G. *Myth and Religion in the Far North*, 1964.

UNITED PRESBYTERIAN: *Intolerance Reviewed*, by "a United Presbyterian", Dumbarton 1858.

U.P.CHURCH: *Rules and Forms of Procedure of the United Presbyterian Church*, Edinburgh 1883.

VINCENT, J.: *The Foundation of the British Liberal Party* (1966), 1972.

WEBSTER, D.: *The History of the Kirkwall United Presbyterian Congregation*, Kirkwall 1910.

WELD, C.R.: *Two Months in the Highlands, Orcadia and Skye*, 1860.

WILSON, J.: *Tales and Travels of a School Inspector*, Glasgow 1928.

# INDEX

176